get decorating

get decorating

beautify your home with paint, wallpaper, floorcoverings and tiles

Consultant

John McGowan

Authors

Mike Collins, David Holloway, Brenda Legge, Diane Carr

Special Photography

Colin Bowling

southwater

This edition is published by Southwater

Southwater is an imprint of Anness Publishing Ltd
Hermes House, 88–89 Blackfriars Road, London SE1 8HA
tel. 020 7401 2077; fax 020 7633 9499
www.southwaterbooks.com; info@anness.com

This edition distributed in the UK by The Manning Partnership Ltd
6 The Old Dairy, Melcombe Road, Bath BA2 3LR
tel. 01225 478 444; fax 01225 478 440; sales@manning-partnership.co.uk

This edition distributed in the USA and Canada by National Book Network
4501 Forbes Boulevard, Suite 200, Lanham, MD 20706
tel. 301 459 3366; fax 301 429 5746; www.nbnbooks.com

This edition distributed in Australia by Pan Macmillan Australia
Level 18, St Martins Tower, 31 Market St, Sydney, NSW 2000
tel. 1300 135 113; fax 1300 135 103; customer.service@macmillan.com.au

This edition distributed in New Zealand by The Five Mile Press (NZ) Ltd
PO Box 33–1071 Takapuna, Unit 11/101–111 Diana Drive, Glenfield, Auckland 10
tel. (09) 444 4144; fax (09) 444 4518; fivemilenz@xtra.co.nz

A CIP catalogue record for this book is available from the British Library.

Publisher: Joanna Lorenz
Managing editor: Judith Simons
Project editor: Felicity Forster
Editor: Ian Penberthy
Designer: Paul Calver
Illustrator: Peter Bull
Photographer: Colin Bowling
Photography consultant: Simon Gilham
Technical assistant: John Ireland
Production controller: Nick Thompson

Previously published as part of a larger volume, *Do-It-Yourself*

1 3 5 7 9 10 8 6 4 2

Publisher's note
The authors and the publisher have made every effort to ensure that all instructions contained in this book are accurate
and safe, and cannot accept liability for any resulting injury, damage or loss to persons or property, however it may arise.
If in doubt as to the correct procedure to follow for any home improvements task, seek professional advice.

Contents

INTRODUCTION

Whether you are faced with a fairly simple decorating job, such as painting a ceiling, or something far more ambitious, such as the complete renovation of all the rooms in a newly purchased home, the same approach to the work is needed. The entire task must be planned thoroughly so that you can be sure of achieving a professional-looking result.

THE PERSONAL TOUCH

Houses and apartments, converted barns and tiny studios are, on their own, merely structures of wood, glass, concrete, masonry and plaster. They come to life only when the personality of the occupant is stamped upon them. Where you live should be how you live; it is more than just a place to eat and sleep. It should be a microcosm of your whole lifestyle in terms of created space, room design, colour schemes, furniture, lighting, garden layout and all that goes with loving and caring for the home.

For this to be true, we need to put in a lot of time thinking about, experimenting with, and enhancing our own environments, and much of this is possible with relatively few skills. Of those skills, decorating techniques – painting, papering, tiling and laying flooring – are the easiest to learn and also the easiest means of making your mark. This book will show you all the techniques you need to do just that.

MASTERING THE SKILLS

Without doubt, painting is the easiest of all the decorating skills to master and it requires little by the way of tools, but it should not be dismissed as simple. Choosing the right type of paint for the application is essential for long-term success, and there are techniques of painting to learn if you want to achieve the best results. Moreover, there is a range of special paint effects that you can experiment with to produce unique finishes and colour combinations.

ABOVE Painting is a great way to stamp your personality on to a room, using the walls and ceilings to create a backdrop that emphasizes the form of furnishings or to make a statement in their own right. The choice of colours and finishes is vast.

Although not as popular as it was once, wallpapering has much to offer in terms of colour, pattern and texture. There is a very wide range of wallcoverings to choose from, not all of them paper-based, which means that you will be able to find something for just about any room in the house. That includes bathrooms, kitchens and children's rooms, where durability, moisture

LEFT Following the sequence for hanging wallpaper should give you little trouble.

resistance and washability are prime requirements. Paper hanging is a definite craft, particularly where heavily patterned types are concerned, but if care is taken it will be possible to achieve far more impressive results than are possible with paint alone.

Tiling is the most difficult of all the decorating techniques when it comes to achieving a professional finish, but ceramic tiles provide essential hard-wearing, waterproof surfaces for bathrooms and kitchens, and the work is not beyond the abilities of a careful, determined amateur. Fortunately, there are many products available to make tiling easier for the do-it-yourselfer, while the range of tiles themselves is vast.

Floorcoverings come in many different forms – carpet, vinyl in sheet and tile form, ceramic and cork tiles, and wood boards and panels – some of which are easier than others to lay. However, none of them should be considered a "no go" area for the do-it-yourselfer. Flooring plays a major part in the appearance of a room and can make or break the effect of your decor, so taking care when choosing the type and colour and/or pattern is essential. Always consider durability

and maintenance too; some floors in your home will receive much more wear than others.

GROUNDWORK

Regardless of the type of decorating job you want to do, good preparation of surfaces is essential. If the surface is in poor condition or sub-standard in any way before you begin, you will never achieve a good result. So spend time on making good. This can often be the most difficult part of a job, and will almost certainly be the most tedious, but in the long term it is always worth the effort.

The major advantage of do-it-yourself is that your time is free, so never rush a job; haste encourages mistakes, leads to disappointment, and can be expensive in the cost of spoiled materials.

UNEXPECTED BONUSES

The money saved in doing your own decorating is an obvious advantage and, in a healthy property market, can help create an asset that grows over the years. For many people, the physical nature of do-it-yourself work also makes a welcome change from a sedentary job. Doing something practical with your hands, and seeing the results

ABOVE FAR LEFT Ragging is one of many paint effects that can produce eye-catching results.

ABOVE LEFT Laying mosaic tiles allows you to enjoy the lustrous beauty of a real wood floor.

ABOVE Four blue ceramic tiles make a good choice for a simple bathroom splashback.

BELOW Paint exterior doors sparingly with high-gloss enamel for a hardwearing finish.

take shape before your eyes, can bring a profound sense of satisfaction and a lasting pride in your environment.

EQUIPMENT AND MATERIALS

To achieve the best results from any do-it-yourself task, it is crucial to make sure you have all the equipment and materials you need, before you begin. Many of the tools and products now available are designed specifically with the amateur enthusiast in mind, and even many traditional materials are now more user-friendly than they once were – all of which can help make your task easier, safer, more enjoyable and ultimately more successful.

SAFETY EQUIPMENT

A complete book could be devoted to the subject of safety in the home, and there is a wide range of equipment designed to minimize our capacity for hurting ourselves. Nevertheless, there is one requirement that we cannot buy, without which all that equipment is virtually useless, namely concentration. This is particularly important when working alone.

AWARENESS

Concentration is essential when using any form of power tool, especially a saw, where one slip can mean the loss of a finger, or worse. The dangers of accidents involving electricity are well documented, as are those involving falls from ladders, spillages of toxic materials, and burns and injuries caused by contact with fire or abrasive surfaces. In almost every case, there is a loss of concentration, coupled with poor work practices and inadequate protective clothing or equipment. So, although the items shown here are all useful, concentrating on what you are doing is the best advice to prevent accidents from occurring around the home and workshop.

BASIC EQUIPMENT

Overalls are a good investment because they not only protect clothing, but also most are designed to be close-fitting to prevent accidental contact with moving machinery. Industrial gloves,

ABOVE Rubber knee pads for floor work avoid damage to both the floor and person.

LEFT The "bump" cap is more stylish than the hard hat and will cope with most accidents.

although not worn by those engaged in fine work, can provide very useful protection against cuts and bruises when doing rougher jobs, such as fencing and garden work. Similarly, safety boots should be worn when heavy lifting or the use of machinery is involved. They are essential when using a chainsaw.

Knee pads are necessary for comfort when laying a floor, stripping one for varnishing or carrying out any other job that requires a lot of kneeling. They will also protect the wearer from injury if a nail or similar projection is knelt on accidentally. Finally, a bump cap is worth considering. This will protect the head from minor

FAR LEFT Wear overalls for protection when painting and decorating.

ABOVE LEFT Gloves are essential when handling rough materials.

LEFT Safety boots with steel toe caps will protect your feet.

injuries and bumps, but is not so cumbersome as the hard hat required on building sites.

It is inevitable that minor cuts and abrasions will occur at some point so a basic first aid kit is another essential for the home or workshop.

AIRBORNE DANGERS

When you are working with wood, the most common airborne danger is dust, mainly from sawing and sanding. This can do long-term damage to the lungs. Many do-it-yourself enthusiasts do not do enough work to warrant a workshop dust extractor, but it would be worth considering if funds allowed. Such a device can be wall-mounted or portable. In the latter case, it can be moved around the house or workshop to suit any tool in use.

A simple face mask, however, will offer adequate protection for occasional jobs. These can also be purchased for protection against fumes, such as from solvents, which can be very harmful. Dust, of course, also affects the eyes, so it is worth investing in a pair of impact-resistant goggles, which will protect the wearer from both fine dust and

LEFT Keeping a basic first aid kit is a common and wise precaution even before any do-it-yourself work is envisaged. It should always be prominently displayed for people unfamiliar with the workshop.

flying debris. Full facial protection is available in the form of a powered respirator for those working in dusty conditions over long periods.

Excessive noise is another airborne pollutant that can be dangerous over a long period. Woodworking machinery, such as planers and circular saws, is often the culprit. Earplugs are the simplest solution and can be left in the ears over a long period. If you need to be able to hear between short bouts of working, ear protectors are the

answer. These can be worn in conjunction with other facial protection quite easily.

PRACTICAL TIP

• Perhaps the most basic advice is to never work alone with machinery and if it is possible always have a friend or colleague nearby to help. If there is no telephone, having a mobile (cell) phone is handy in the workshop.

ABOVE Ear defenders are good for really loud noise, and are easy to take on and off.

ABOVE Dust extraction is the first line of defence in the workshop.

ABOVE A simple face mask can filter out the worst dust pollution.

ELECTRICAL AND LADDER SAFETY

Most safety considerations concerning the use of power tools will be set out by the manufacturers in the operating instructions, so it is essential always to read the manuals on purchase and follow these to the letter. Using ladders, however, needs some direct input from the user by way of common sense, since no two situations are ever the same.

ELECTRICAL SAFETY

Some tools have removable switches that allow the user to immobilize the tool and prevent any unauthorized use. Provisions for the use of padlocks are also common on machinery, and it is wise to buy tools with such facilities.

To safeguard against electrocution, which can occur if the flex (power cord) is faulty or is cut accidentally, the ideal precaution is a residual current device (RCD). This is simply plugged into the main supply socket (electrical outlet) before the flex and will give complete protection to the user. Extension leads (power cords) can be purchased with automatic safety cut-outs and insulated sockets and are ideal for both outside and inside work.

The danger of electrocution or damage caused by accidentally drilling into an existing cable or pipe can be largely prevented by using an electronic pipe and cable detector, which will locate and differentiate between metal pipes, wooden studs and live wires through plaster or concrete to a depth of approximately 50mm (2in). These are not too expensive and will be very useful around the home.

The danger of fire is ever present in both the home and workshop, so a fire extinguisher (possibly two or three) is necessary for every do-it-yourself enthusiast. It should be wall-mounted in plain view and tested and serviced regularly.

ABOVE AND LEFT Pipe and cable detectors give information which can largely eliminate any danger from electrocution.

ABOVE Proper cable reels and insulated sockets protect the user from electrocution.

LEFT A simple circuit breaker can save a life.

ABOVE A fire extinguisher is absolutely essential in the workshop or at home. Make sure the one you have is adequate for the size and type of workshop, and the type of fire source.

ABOVE A ladder platform will ensure a firm footing, especially if heavy footwear is worn.

SLIPPING AND FALLING

Steps and ladders can be hazardous, so make sure they are in good condition. Accessories to make a ladder safer to use include the roof hook, which slips over the ridge for safety; the ladder stay, which spreads the weight of the ladder across a vertical surface, such as a wall to prevent slippage; and the standing platform, which is used to provide a more comfortable and safer surface to stand on. The last often has a ribbed rubber surface and can be attached to the rungs of almost all ladders. Even more stable is the moveable workstation or a board or staging slung between two pairs of steps or trestles. These can often be used with a safety rail, which prevents the operator from falling even if a slip occurs.

ABOVE RIGHT A moveable workstation simplifies the whole process.

RIGHT Platforms supported by trestles are the safest way to paint from a height.

RIGHT Keeping tools on a stable surface when working at heights adds to your personal safety.

BELOW RIGHT A ladder attachment over the ridge of a roof improves safety and avoids damage to the roof covering.

BELOW Make sure that your ladder is secure at ground level. This is one of the most important steps to safe working practice.

PAINTING EQUIPMENT

This is one aspect of do-it-yourself work where you cannot afford to skimp on materials. You will not achieve professional results by using cheap brushes that shed their bristles as you work, or cut-price rollers that disintegrate before the job is finished. Invest in the best quality equipment your budget allows if you are serious about your work.

CHOOSING BRUSHES

Paintbrushes come in pure bristle, synthetic fibre and even foam versions. The last guarantees that you will not be left with brush strokes, and they are inexpensive enough to discard when you have finished. All natural brushes shed a few bristles in use, but cheap brushes are the worst offenders. Usually, these have fewer bristles to start with and they are often poorly secured. Regard pure bristle brushes as an investment; you can reuse them repeatedly, and many professional painters claim that their performance improves with age.

Synthetic brushes, usually with nylon bristles, have the big advantage of being moult-free, and they perform well with water-based paints. A more expensive version, made of polyester and nylon, is particularly easy to handle and said to give a superior finish.

TOOL BOX ESSENTIALS

Serious painters will need a range of brushes: slimline, 12 and 25mm (½ and 1in), for fiddly areas, such as window frames; medium sized versions, 50 and 75mm (2 and 3in), for doors, floors and skirting (base) boards; and large types, 100mm (4in), for quick coverage of walls and ceilings. You might like to add a few extras to this basic kit:
- A cutting-in (sash) brush, specially angled to cope with hard-to-reach areas, is particularly useful if you are painting around window frames. It comes in 12mm, 18mm and 25mm (½, ¾ and 1in) versions.

PRACTICAL TIPS

- Work new brushes across your palm to dislodge any loose bristles.

- Use an extension pole with your roller when painting ceilings.

- Imagine you are holding a pen when using lightweight brushes; this gives maximum control.

- A radiator brush, available with a plastic or metal handle and designed to reach the wall behind a radiator.
- Special-effects brushes, from stubby stencil brushes to mottlers, which allow you to create the distinctive look of woodgrain, and a range of artist's brushes for adding detail.

100mm (4in) brush

75mm (3in)

50mm (2in)

25mm (1in)

12mm (½in)

Dragging and colourwash brushes

Foam brushes

Stippling brush

Stencil brush and artist's brushes

Metal and plastic-handled radiator brushes

PAINT PADS

If you are new to decorating, you may find that a paint pad is easier to handle than a brush. It gives a speedy and even finish, is light to handle and works particularly well with acrylic paints. Experiment with a single pad first before investing in a kit, to make sure you are happy with the tool.

Each pad consists of a layer of fibre on top of a layer of foam, which in turn is attached to a plastic handle. Use paint pads in conjunction with a paint tray. If you purchase a kit, a tray will usually be provided.

THE RIGHT ROLLER

If speed is of the essence, a paint roller will be an indispensable part of your decorating kit. Once you have purchased a roller, you can simply buy replacement sleeves that fit the existing handle.

Use sleeves with a short pile for smooth surfaces and for applying gloss paint. Medium-pile sleeves work well on smooth and lightly-textured surfaces, and with standard and solid emulsion (latex) paint. Use long-pile sleeves on uneven and textured surfaces.

ABOVE FAR LEFT Use a cutting-in brush on a window frame.

ABOVE LEFT Load paint on to the paint pad using the tray supplied with the pad.

ABOVE Use a power roller to paint large areas.

Power rollers are mains or battery-operated and in theory they can simplify the whole process, with the paint contained in a portable reservoir. However, they can result in drips and streaks, and many professional decorators prefer more conventional methods.

Paint pads

Cutting-in brush

Long-, medium- and short-pile roller sleeves

Roller handle

TYPES OF PAINT

Today, there are so many different shades, textures, and thicknesses of paint to choose from that making the right choice can seem bewildering. In reality, having more choice can make the job easier. Whether you are painting your house interior: kitchen, bathroom, lounge, ceiling, floor; or exterior: shed, conservatory, fences, decking, drainpipes, there is a paint to meet your needs.

DIFFERENT TYPES OF PAINT

All paints fall into one of two broad categories: water- or oil-based. Emulsions (latex) paints fit into the first category and are typically used on walls and ceilings. Oil-based paints, such as glosses and enamels, contain a solvent and they are ideal for wood surfaces such as doors, skirting (base) boards and window frames, and any metalwork. Both water- and oil-based paints come in matt (flat), mid-sheen (semi-gloss) and full gloss finishes.

If you are using emulsion paint, you will not need a separate under-coat, but you will need to apply at least two coats for good coverage. In general, gloss and enamel paints do require a separate undercoat, unless of the one-coat variety. One-coat emulsions are particularly useful when painting ceilings, reducing the amount of work involved.

Remember that if you are working with bare wood, metal, concrete or stone surfaces, you will need to apply a primer before the undercoat.

PAINT CONSISTENCY

The thickness of paint is influenced by various additives. When thinning paint make sure you use the correct diluent. At one end of the spectrum are fully-liquid paints, which require a certain amount of expertise to ensure a drip-free finish; at the other are non-drip, thixotropic or solid paints, which give a good finish whatever your skill level. Use them at cornice-level, on ceilings and above picture rails to avoid splashes.

ABOVE 1 powder pigments, 2 emulsion (latex) paints, 3 acrylic primer, 4 artist's acrylic colours, 5 acrylic scumble, 6 crackle glaze, 7 neutral wax, 8 methylated spirit (denatured alcohol), 9 brown shellac, 10 clear shellac.

BELOW FAR LEFT A selection of different-coloured paints, including watercolours, stencil paints and acrylics.

BELOW LEFT Before using, stir liquid paints with a wooden stick.

BELOW One-coat paints rapidly speed up paint decorating tasks.

SPECIAL PAINTS

Textured paints produce a relief pattern on internal walls and ceilings. They are best applied with a roller, which can be plain or have a textured patterned sleeve.

Enamel radiator paints are designed to withstand high temperatures and will not discolour like ordinary paints. You can choose from a range of bright colours to suit your decor, in satin or gloss.

Floor paints can enliven the dullest expanse of concrete, stone or wood. There is even a variety to transform tired vinyl and linoleum floors. Vary the effect with stripes, geometrical shapes or stencils for a unique look.

Kitchen and bathroom paints are specially formulated to cope with damp conditions. They contain a fungicide to stop mould growth and are considerably tougher than standard emulsions.

Microporous paints are also known as "breathing" paints. These water-based finishes, which are typically used on exterior wood, will expand

RIGHT Traditional, or historic, paints are the perfect choice for period houses.

FAR RIGHT Fence paints come in a wide colour range and give a weatherproof finish.

and contract with the timber. These paints also let moisture escape so you will not end up with flaky or blistered paint surfaces.

The range of special paints is growing by the day. There are paints for use on MDF (medium-density fiberboard) and melamine surfaces, plus tried and tested outdoor paints, including masonry paints for rendered surfaces, colourful garden paints for walls, containers, fences and sheds, bituminous paints for pipes and guttering, and security paints, which remain tacky to prevent would-be felons from entering the house by climbing the drainpipes.

There are also traditional paints that use authentic materials; they come in various finishes, including matt, distemper, eggshell and gloss.

ABOVE FAR LEFT Textured paints are excellent for covering minor flaws in plasterwork.

ABOVE LEFT Turn off the heating, and allow the radiator to cool before applying paint.

ABOVE Start at the innermost corner and work outward when painting floors.

PRACTICAL TIPS

• On freshly plastered walls, make sure you use a new-plaster emulsion; standard types will not allow the plaster to dry out fully.

• If the paint can you are using is still quite full, seal it, upend it to allow the paint to form a protective seal around the lid. Store the can upside down until you need it.

Wallpapering Equipment

Using the correct tools will make the job of hanging wallpaper much easier, allowing you to achieve a more professional finish. Some are needed specifically for wallpapering; others are likely to be part of your standard do-it-yourself tool kit. When buying decorating tools, opt for quality rather than quantity – to make sure they last longer and produce better results.

Measuring and marking

A retractable steel tape is essential for taking accurate measurements, while a long metal straightedge, a spirit level and a pencil will be needed for marking levels, vertical guidelines on walls and the positions of fixtures.

Cutting and trimming

For cutting wallpaper to length and trimming edges, you will need a pair of paperhanger's scissors, which have long blades and curved tips used for creasing paper into angles. Choose scissors that are at least 250mm (10in) long and made from stainless steel, or have been specially coated so that they will not rust.

A sharp craft knife can also be used for trimming and will be easier to use with vinyl wallcoverings. Various trimming tools are also available, including the roller cutter, which enables you to crease and cut into edges with a single movement, and is accurate and simple to use.

Pasting

For mixing and applying paste, you will need a plastic bucket and a paste brush. Proper paste brushes have synthetic bristles and will be easier to clean than ordinary paintbrushes. A pasting table is not essential, but is extremely useful. They are also inexpensive and fold for easy storage. For ready-pasted wallcoverings, a polystyrene soaking trough is required.

ABOVE A paste table is not essential, but will make the job of pasting and hanging wallcoverings much easier. Also shown are the essentials for mixing and applying paste. Keep a decorator's sponge handy to wipe away traces of adhesive on the wallcovering or paste table.

ABOVE A polystyrene trough is needed for soaking ready-pasted wallcoverings. This will allow you to carry each drop to where it will be hung, and help to keep water off the floor.

Avoiding paste drips

A length of string tied tightly across the top of a wallpaper paste bucket makes a handy brush rest. Use the string rather than the side of the bucket for removing excess adhesive from the pasting brush.

ABOVE Take accurate measurements with a retractable steel tape.

BELOW A plumbline provides a vertical guideline for hanging the first length of wallpaper on each wall.

ABOVE A sharp craft knife is useful for making awkward cuts, and trimming vinyl wallcoverings.

ABOVE Use spirit levels to ensure that wallcoverings are hung straight, and pattern repeats are level.

LEFT Paperhanger's scissors have very long blades, making it much easier to cut wallpaper neatly.

BELOW A decorator's sponge holds water well and is good for washing down walls.

BELOW A soft-bristle paperhanger's brush is the best tool for smoothing ordinary wallpaper into place.

BELOW A seam roller gives a professional finish to wallpaper seams and the edges of borders, particularly vinyl wallcoverings.

HANGING

To ensure that wallpaper is hung straight and true, a plumbline or spirit level are essential. Hanging wallpaper may also involve working at heights, so access equipment will be required. A set of sturdy steps will be suitable for papering walls, but a safe work platform will be needed for ceilings and stairwells.

FINISHING

A paperhanger's brush is the best tool for smoothing down wallpaper, although a sponge can be used for vinyl wallcoverings. For the best results, choose a brush with soft, flexible bristles and buy the largest size that you can manage comfortably. Do not use wallpaper brushes with a metal ferrule or collar on them for this job, as you might inadvertently tear or mark delicate wallcoverings.

Use a cellulose decorator's sponge rather than an ordinary household sponge. This type of sponge is made of a higher-density material, which is firmer and will hold water better. It can also be used for washing down walls before papering or painting.

A seam roller will give a neat finish to joints and the edges of borders, but should not be used on wallpaper with an embossed pattern. Various types made from wood and plastic are available. A soft plastic seam roller is the best option as it is less likely to leave marks on thin or overpasted wallpapers.

TYPES OF WALLCOVERING

When choosing wallcoverings, it is important to take into consideration how practical it will be in the room you wish to decorate. Each room in your home has very different requirements and by choosing the right type of wallcovering, you will be sure of a decorative surface that will wear well and look good for years to come.

LINING PAPER

This provides a smooth base for wallpaper or paint on walls and ceilings. It is made in several grades from light 480 grade, suitable for new or near perfect walls, to extra-thick 1200 grade for use on rough and pitted plaster. A good-quality lining paper will be easier to handle than a cheap, thin paper and less likely to tear when pasted.

WALLPAPERS FOR PAINTING

Woodchip paper is made by sandwiching particles of wood between two layers of paper. The thicker grades are easy to hang and cover uneven surfaces well, but woodchip is not easy to cut and can be difficult to remove, while the thinner grades tear easily. Woodchip is a budget-buy, but not particularly attractive or durable.

Relief wallpaper is imprinted with a raised, decorative surface pattern and is available in a wide choice of designs, as well as pre-cut dado (chair rail) panels and borders. It is quite easy to hang, although the thinner grades can tear when wet. It hides blemishes well and is durable once painted.

Textured vinyl has a deeply embossed surface pattern that masks

ABOVE Some wallcoverings are more hardwearing than others. Bear this in mind when choosing a pattern and material.

Lining paper

Woodchip paper

Paint-over relief wallpaper

Textured vinyl wallcovering

Heavy-duty embossed wallcovering

flaws and is uncrushable, so it is suitable for hardwearing areas such as the hall (lobby) and children's rooms. It is more expensive than relief wallpaper, but very easy to hang and usually dry strippable.

Embossed wallcovering comes in rolls and pre-cut panels made from a solid film of linseed oil and fillers fused on to a backing paper. It requires a special adhesive and will crack if folded, but it is not difficult to hang. It is very expensive, but is extremely hardwearing and durable, and the deeply-profiled, traditional designs are well suited to older and period properties.

PATTERNED WALLCOVERINGS

Printed wallpaper is available in an extensive choice of patterns and colours. The cheapest are machine-printed, but top-price designs are hand-printed and often untrimmed, so hanging is best left to the professionals. Printed wallpaper can be sponged, but is not particularly durable and is best used in rooms where it will not be subjected to much wear. The thinner grades tear easily when pasted.

Washable wallpaper also comes in a good choice of designs, but is more durable and has a thin plastic coating that allows the surface to be washed clean. It is priced competitively, fairly easy to hang and in some cases is dry strippable.

Vinyl wallcovering has a very durable surface layer of PVC that creates a hardwearing, often scrubbable, finish that resists steam, moisture and mould. There is a good choice of colours and patterns, as well as pearlized and embossed textured designs. Vinyl wallcovering is usually ready-pasted and dry strippable; paste-the-wall ranges are also available.

Sculptured vinyl is a thick, very hardwearing vinyl imprinted with a decorative design or tile effect. The waterproof finish resists steam, condensation, grease and cooking splashes, so it is a good choice for kitchens and bathrooms. It requires a heavy-duty adhesive, but is easy to hang and is dry strippable.

SPECIAL WALLCOVERINGS

Metallic foils and wallcoverings made from natural materials such as cork, silk and grasscloth can often be ordered from dedicated decorating outlets. They are expensive and difficult to hang, so employing a professional is advisable. In general, they are hard to clean, so they are best for low-wear areas of the home.

Printed wallpaper

Vinyl wallcovering

Paste-the-wall wallcovering

Sculptured vinyl wallcovering

Special metallic wallcoverings

Floorcoverings

Whether you have a solid concrete floor or a suspended timber floor, there is a wide range of floorcoverings to choose from. Floorcoverings can be divided into five main groups, including carpet; sheet materials, mainly vinyl and linoleum; soft floor tiles including vinyl, cork, rubber, linoleum and carpet tiles; hard floor tiles such as ceramic and quarry tiles; and timber floors.

Carpet

There are two main types of carpet: fabric-backed and foam-backed. The former requires special edge gripper strips and an underlay, and is difficult for an amateur to lay successfully, as it has to be stretched as it is laid. The latter requires no underlay, except paper to cover gaps in floorboards, and is easy to cut and to lay, using double-sided adhesive tape.

Carpet comes in a vast range of designs and qualities, and in different grades for a variety of situations: the heaviest wear grades are required in hallways and on stairs; the lowest grades in bedrooms. Water-resistant grades are needed in bathrooms. Carpet, except carpet tiles, is not recommended for kitchens.

Sheet materials

Vinyl sheet flooring is easy to cut, easy to lay and easy to keep clean, making it ideal for use in bathrooms, kitchens and children's bedrooms.

LEFT A linoleum floor is ideal for kitchens as it is very durable and easy to keep clean. The cushioned types also offer extra warmth and softness underfoot. Borders can be used to frame individual tiles.

Normal sheet vinyl is reasonably soft and warm underfoot, cushion vinyl even more so.

Durable linoleum (oil-impregnated sheet) is the traditional sheet flooring, but is more difficult to lay. However, modern linos come in a range of patterns and colourful designs that rival vinyl sheeting.

Soft floor tiles

All soft floor tiles are quiet, warm and comfortable underfoot. As they are also easy to clean, they are suitable for bathrooms, kitchens work rooms and bedrooms.

All soft floor tile materials must be laid on a surface that is absolutely dry and flat: a solid concrete floor

ABOVE A variety of natural floor-coverings such as sea grass.

ABOVE Carpet tiles can be laid with any pattern.

ABOVE A selection of soft floor-coverings, including cork.

ABOVE There is a vast array of hard flooring tiles available.

will probably require levelling, while a timber floor may need covering with sheets of hardboard.

Most soft floor tiles are laid in the same way. Individual tiles are stuck to the floor using the correct adhesive or by peeling off the backing from self-adhesive tiles. In general, carpet tiles are laid dry, with perhaps just a few secured with double-sided adhesive tape to keep the whole floor in place.

HARD FLOOR TILES

These materials are also easy to keep clean, so they can be used in the same rooms as soft floor tiles. They are much more durable, but are cold underfoot and noisy.

The main materials are ceramic (glazed clay), and quarry or terracotta. Ceramic floor tiles, which are thicker and stronger than ceramic wall tiles, are laid with a special adhesive, and grout is used to fill the gaps between them. Quarry and terracotta tiles are laid with a cement mortar, which is also used to fill the gaps. Hard floor tiles need a rigid, dry, flat surface. On a timber floor, this means laying thin plywood sheeting rather than hardboard.

LEFT Quarry tiles are unglazed ceramic floor tiles with a brown, buff or reddish colour, and are a very popular choice for hallways, conservatories and country-style kitchens. Terracotta tiles are featured here.

TIMBER FLOORCOVERINGS

There are many timber floorcoverings that can be laid on top of existing floors. Some are nailed down, some are stuck down and some are allowed to "float", not actually being secured to the floor underneath, but being free to expand and contract independently.

Timber flooring is available in thin strips, sometimes two or three boards wide, resembling floorboards. The strips are tongued and grooved and are glued together, but not to the floor underneath. Thicker timber strips can be laid in the same way, but can also be nailed to the floor below. Although some thick strips are made of hardwood, this timber is so expensive that in some cases, laminate flooring (a thin hardwood layer attached to a thick softwood layer) is used. Timber mosaic flooring, often known as imitation parquet flooring, consists of square tiles that

are glued to the underlying floor; most types are self-adhesive. Each tile consists of four smaller tiles, and each smaller tile comprises a number of small timber "fingers", so the final effect is a basketweave design. True parquet flooring consists of thick blocks that are glued to the floor, typically using a black mastic (caulking), in a herringbone pattern. Achieving a flat level surface with this type of flooring is not easy. Timber floorboards themselves can be made to look good if varnished.

LEFT Woodstrip, laminated and mosaic flooring.

RIGHT A wooden floor can be warm and stylish.

TILING EQUIPMENT

Tiles used for wall decoration are generally fairly thin, measuring 4–6mm (³⁄₁₆–¼in) thick, although some imported tiles (especially the larger sizes) may be rather thicker than this. Floor tiles are thicker and harder to cut, and require more heavy-duty adhesive and grout than those sold for walls, so make sure you buy the correct materials for the job.

TILING TOOLS

For almost any ceramic tiling job, large or small, a good selection of tools will simplify the whole process.

A tile file makes light work of smoothing cut edges. A tile saw is useful for making shaped cuts to fit around obstacles such as pipework. Choose the coarse variety of abrasive paper for rubbing down paintwork. An all-in-one tile cutter, or tile jig, will make life easier for a beginner. Most incorporate a measuring device, trimmer and snapping mechanism in one neat unit. A standard tile cutter works well, but requires practice for best results.

Tile spacers are required when using standard field tiles. Other types have bevelled edges that create a grouting gap automatically when butted together.

A chinagraph (wax) pencil is suitable for marking glazed surfaces such as tiles. The marks are easy to erase when the job is finished.

A notched adhesive spreader will create a series of ridges in the adhesive, allowing it to spread when the tile is pressed home and ensuring that an even thickness of adhesive is applied. A squeegee will be needed at the grouting stage to force grout into the gaps between tiles.

Additions to this basic list are a spirit level for setting out horizontal and vertical guidelines; a straight-edge and tape measure; a sponge for

cleaning off excess adhesive or applying grout; tile nippers for cutting off small pieces of tile; a glass cutter for cutting mirror tiles; a tile saw for cutting out complex shapes; and a pointing trowel for spreading adhesive. You will also need a tiling gauge for working out the positioning of tiles, made of lengths of softwood battening.

Snap-off tile file

Tile edge sander with abrasive strips

2mm (¹⁄₁₆in) tile spacers

Grout absorbent sponge

Pointed tiling trowel

Notched spreader

Squeegee

Chinagraph pencil

ADHESIVE AND GROUT

Both adhesive and grout for tiling are now usually sold ready-mixed in plastic tubs complete with a notched plastic spreader for your convenience. For areas that will get the occasional splash or may suffer from condensation, a water-resistant adhesive and grout is perfectly adequate, but for surfaces such as shower cubicles and around baths, which will have to withstand prolonged wetting, it is essential to use both waterproof adhesive and waterproof grout.

Always use waterproof grout on tiled worktops; ordinary grout will harbour germs. Some silicone sealant or mastic (caulking) may also be needed for waterproofing joints where tiling abuts, such as on baths, basins and shower trays.

It is important that you allow adhesive to dry for at least 24 hours before applying grout.

GROUTING

This is generally white, but coloured grout is on sale and will make a feature of the grout lines (an effect that looks best with plain or fairly neutral patterned tiles).

Adhesive and grout are both sold in a range of quantities, sometimes labelled by weight, sometimes by volume. Always check the coverage specified by the manufacturer on the packaging when buying, so as not to buy too much or run out halfway through the job.

TOOLS FOR ADHESIVE AND GROUTING

Notched spreaders are used for creating a series of ridges in the adhesive, allowing it to spread when the tile is pressed home, and ensuring that an even thickness of adhesive is applied. They are available in various sizes. Grouting tools include a grout spreader, grout finisher and grout remover.

Tile saw

Mosaic nippers

Tile cutter with jaws

Grout refinishing kit

Grout remover and tile scorer (above)

Straightedge

Heavy-duty tile cutter with jaws

Tile jig with adjustable width and angle facility

PAINTING AND WALLPAPERING

It is possible to completely transform your home by using paint and wallpaper – the choice of colours and patterns is immense, and it is not difficult to obtain great results. Paying attention to preparation and detail in the early stages is the key to success.

PAINT PREPARATION

Proper groundwork is essential for decorating. Never be tempted to cut corners, as the results will be disappointing. Indeed, preparatory work may sometimes take longer than the time spent on painting, but by paying attention to detail in the early stages the whole decorating process will be made much easier and you will achieve a more professional finish.

PREPARATION

Start by giving yourself room to manoeuvre. Clear the room of as much furniture as possible, pack away ornaments, and remove curtains, shelves, mirrors and pictures. Large items of furniture should be moved to the middle of the room and covered with dust sheets (drop cloths) to protect them from splashes.

Use masking tape to protect light switches and the like from paint droplets, and cover radiators with dust sheets. Old bed sheets are good for protecting the floor; plastic dust sheets should be avoided, as it is easy to slip on them. Keep all your tools and equipment close to hand as a lot of time can be wasted if you need to make excursions to other rooms to find essentials. It will also help to choose a stepladder with an integral tray for holding paint cans and small tools. Alternatively, you can buy a clip-on metal hook to hold a paint can securely.

ABOVE Use masking tape to protect light switches and fittings from paint splashes.

BASIC PROCEDURES

For the best results, surfaces to be painted must be clean, even and blemish-free. If plasterwork is damaged beyond repair, you may have to consider a professional replastering job. New plasterwork must be allowed to dry for at least four to five weeks, then a plaster primer or PVA adhesive (white glue) thinned with water should be applied before the area can be decorated. If a new-plaster emulsion (latex) paint is used, painting can take place almost immediately.

Plasterboard (gypsum board) surfaces should be primed initially, or painted with a thinned coat of emulsion paint before applying the top coat. Cracks and gaps in plasterwork must be filled with a general-purpose filler. Apply it so that it is slightly proud of the surface, then sand smooth when dry. Tiny cracks and scratches will

ABOVE Keep all your tools and equipment close to your work area.

usually disappear when you apply a standard emulsion. Tackle large holes by applying the filler in a series of layers, allowing each to dry before applying the next one.

PRACTICAL TIPS

• Always wear safety goggles when you are cleaning ceilings to prevent any detergent from splashing into your eyes.

• Old properties may have been decorated with lead paint. Take great care when removing this finish. Never use a heat gun to strip off lead paint. For safety, use wet abrasive paper when sanding down to keep dust levels to a minimum, and wear a face mask.

If you are working on walls that have been painted before, wash them thoroughly with a solution of sugar soap (all-purpose cleaner), then rinse with tepid water and allow to dry. Lightly sand the surface to provide a key before applying the new coat of paint. Clean the ceiling with a long-handled mop and detergent mixed with water. Rinse with clean water.

Scrape off flaking or blistered paint with a wallpaper scraper, then sand lightly and remove all traces of dust before applying a new finish. If there is mould growth on the walls, wash the area with a detergent solution and also treat with a fungicide before painting. If the area remains untreated, stains will soon show through the new paintwork.

Older properties may have been decorated with distemper, which is powdered chalk mixed with water and size. Before over-painting, brush away any dust or debris and seal with a stabilizing primer.

Ideally, all old wallcoverings should be removed before painting. Often, however, sound paper surfaces can be covered successfully. Do not attempt to paint over a vinyl wall-covering: it peels off easily to leave a ready-made lining paper in place. Start at the bottom of each length and loosen the top layer at each corner. Pull the vinyl firmly toward you and work steadily upward, removing as large a section as possible. Remove stubborn fragments of vinyl with a scraper.

LARGE CRACKS

Use a paintbrush to remove dust from large cracks prior to filling, then rinse and work the damp bristles into the crack to promote good adhesion.

ABOVE Ensure filler adheres well in deep cracks or holes with careful preparation.

PREPARING WALLS AND CEILINGS

1 Strip wallcoverings with water or steam and scrapers. Peel off the top layer of vinyl types.

2 Remove flaking paint with a narrow or wide-bladed scraper.

3 Fill any cracks and gaps in plasterwork with all-purpose filler.

4 Sand the filled area smooth when dry with a fine abrasive paper.

5 Give the walls a thorough wash with a solution of sugar soap (all-purpose cleaner).

6 Use a squeegee mop to clean ceilings so that you can work at ground level.

Brushes, Rollers and Pads

Paint, whether water-based or oil-based, can be applied with brushes, rollers and paint pads. Each has its advantages and disadvantages, but all have a place in the decorator's tool kit. It is important to use the correct application techniques in order to get the best out of your equipment. Look after your tools, cleaning and drying them as described here, and they will last for a long time.

Brush techniques

Use a thin, straight piece of wood to stir the paint thoroughly, unless it is a non-drip variety. Decant about a third of the can into a paint kettle (pot), which will be lighter and easier to work with than the can itself. Dip the brush into the paint to about a third of the length of the bristles, and remove any excess by dabbing lightly inside the container. Start at the top of your work area and use light, criss-cross strokes for good coverage when using emulsion (latex) paints. Emulsion paints can dry very rapidly, resulting in hard edges. Work quickly and use the "laying off" technique to prevent this. Simply complete each application with feathery, upward strokes. These should blend into the fresh paint when you start again.

Oil-based paints take longer to dry and require a different technique: start by painting a series of vertical lines, then blend them together with an almost dry brush. This should prevent any joins from showing.

Cleaning brushes

First remove excess paint by scraping the brush with a spatula or knife. Cold water is all you need to remove water-based paints: simply hold brushes under a running tap and wipe clean with a cloth.

Oil-based paints are more difficult to remove. Decant some white spirit (paint thinner) or paint cleaner into a jar and leave the brush to soak. Drilling a hole through the handle

ABOVE Always clean your brushes thoroughly.

allows you to suspend the brush in the white spirit so that the bristles are clear of the sediment that collects in the bottom of the jar. Finally, clean it with soapy water, then rinse well and dry with a cloth.

Using a roller

For speed of application, a paint roller is the natural choice. However, it cannot deal with corner details and edges; you will need to paint these areas with a small brush before tackling the main job. Fit the roller with a suitable sleeve. Then pour a small amount of paint into the deep

Practical tips

• A small roller, typically 100mm (4in) long, is excellent for painting doors and similar areas.

• Aim to complete a whole wall in one session for a seamless, professional look.

section of the roller tray, dip in the roller and run it lightly over the raised section. Do not overload the roller. Apply the paint in a zigzag pattern, keeping the roller in contact with the surface all the time. A common mistake is to let the roller rotate rapidly as you finish a section; this will send out a shower of paint.

Cleaning rollers

First, run the roller over newspaper to remove excess paint. Then use cold running water to remove water-based paints, and white spirit or brush cleaner for solvent-based

Using a paintbrush

1 Dip the first third of the brush in paint, and wipe off the excess.

2 Finish the area of painting with a light, upward stroke.

USING A BRUSH AND ROLLER

1 Use a brush to cut in around the edges of walls and ceilings, where a roller cannot reach.

2 Slide your chosen roller sleeve on to the roller cage.

3 Load the roller with paint and then run it over the raised section.

4 Apply the paint in a zigzag formation and do not lift the roller as you work.

MESS-FREE TRAYS

A easy way of keeping a clean roller tray is to line it with aluminium foil before you use it, then lift it out and discard it when you have finished.

Clean the roller as outlined here and in accordance with the type of paint used and the manufacturer's instructions.

ABOVE Use foil to line the tray and there will be less mess to clear up afterwards.

paints. In the latter case, finish off with soapy water and leave to dry.

PAINTING WITH PADS

Paint pads tend to apply a thinner coat than rollers and brushes, but they give rapid results and are good for covering large areas. Pads are usually sold with their own tray, but

you could pour some paint into a roller tray. If you are using a special pad tray, run the pad over the integral roller. Alternatively, run it over the shallow section of the tray. Wipe off excess paint before you start. Keep the pad in contact with the wall and move it lightly in a criss-cross pattern.

CLEANING PADS

A pad can be cleaned in the same manner as a roller, depending on the type of paint being used. Do not leave it to soak in a jar of brush cleaner or water, however, as the fibre pad could separate from its backing. Store the paint pad in an upright position to dry.

USING A PAINT PAD

1 Apply paint to the paint pad and remove the excess on the integral roller.

2 Use a small paint pad to cut in around the edges of the walls and ceiling.

3 Fill in with a larger pad, applying paint in a criss-cross pattern.

Painting Ceilings and Walls

If you are planning to paint a room completely, there is a logical order to follow. The basic technique is to start at the top and work down, with the exception of cornices, which, if they are to be painted a separate colour, need to be completed at a later stage. By breaking a room into workable sections you will do the job more efficiently and create the minimum of mess and disruption.

Ceilings

For obvious reasons, start with the ceiling to avoid rivulets of paint running down freshly painted walls. Then paint the walls and finally the woodwork, such as window frames and doors. Skirting (base) boards and floors are last on the agenda.

The simplest and quickest way to paint a ceiling is with a roller on an extension pole, allowing you to remain at floor level for the majority of the work. First, however, the edges of the ceiling will need to be cut in with a paintbrush, working from a stepladder.

If you prefer to be nearer the ceiling, a work platform is a good idea. For a reasonable outlay, you can hire a platform and support trestles or a mobile workstation with locking castors that can be moved to wherever you need it. Alternatively, place a strong plank between two stepladders.

LEFT It is best to paint ceilings in bands from one wall to another.

If the original paintwork is sound, wash thoroughly and let it dry. Any staining should be treated at this stage with a primer/sealer. First, paint a border around the perimeter of the ceiling with a small brush. To make the most of the available light, start from a corner close to a window area and work inward.

Paint in strips from one wall to another, then back, working quickly so that the edges do not have time to dry. If you prefer a brush to a roller or pad, make sure that it is at least 100mm (4in) wide. Use a small cutting-in (sash) brush around features such as light fittings and ceiling roses. Complete the work in

ABOVE Platforms supported by trestles are a safe way to paint from a height.

LEFT A moveable workstation simplifies the process of painting ceilings and high walls.

ABOVE Use a small cutting-in (sash) brush to paint around light fittings.

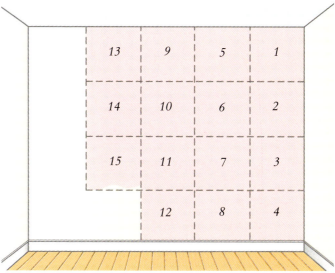

ABOVE LEFT The correct order to paint a room.

ABOVE Mentally divide each wall into a grid and paint one area at a time as shown.

one session to avoid hard paint lines that will show in the finish. Then apply a second coat when the first is dry, unless using a one-coat product.

WALLS

As with the ceiling, start in the lightest corner of the room, working from the top of the wall down. If you are right-handed, begin on the right-hand side of the wall, or the left if you are left-handed.

When you are using a roller, paint horizontal strips across the wall, but still using the zigzag technique, take care to blend them carefully to avoid join marks. With a brush, paint in vertical blocks around 600mm (2ft) square, and complete an entire wall before taking a break.

TEXTURED PAINTS

When walls and ceilings have lumpy or uneven surfaces, consider using a textured paint to hide the irregularities. Essentially thick versions of emulsion (latex) paint, they may tear into delicate foam rollers, so they are best applied with a brush or dense-pile roller. You can buy a range of rollers designed for use with this type of paint to create textured patterns such as diamonds and stripes. On the negative side, textured paint finishes can be difficult to clean and remove.

PRACTICAL TIPS

• Cover your head and wear goggles if you are using a standard emulsion (latex) paint on a ceiling. Alternatively, use a non-drip version to reduce splashes.

• Use colour to create visual illusions in your room. A deep shade on the ceiling will appear to reduce the height, whereas a light shade will have the opposite effect. A dark colour on the walls will make the room seem smaller; a light shade will create the illusion of space.

ABOVE Pale colours, such as blue or pale lilac, can make a room look larger.

ABOVE Textured paint finishes can create a variety of effects.

DECORATIVE PAINT EFFECTS

Why settle for plain, "flat" paintwork, when you can create an attractive effect with a decorative paint finish? The beauty of paint effects is that they can be used on a variety of surfaces, including walls, ceilings, furniture and floors. Even beginners need not feel apprehensive about tackling the most popular techniques, and there are special paints and tools available to make the job easier.

SPONGING

This is a simple technique. It works well with emulsion (latex) paints and oil-based glazes. A natural sponge will give a more subtle effect than a synthetic type.

Begin by applying a base coat with a standard emulsion paint and allow to dry. Soak the sponge in water, then squeeze out as much moisture as possible. Select a second emulsion for the top colour – it is best to choose one that is similar in tone to the base coat. Pour a little of the emulsion into a tray and dip in the sponge. The overall effect should be as subtle as possible, so wipe off any excess paint on the raised area of the tray or a clean sheet of paper.

Start at the top of your work area and begin dabbing paint on to the base colour. Turn the sponge around as you work to vary the effect, aiming for a continuous pattern with no "rivers" of base coat showing through. Once this coat is dry, you can add a second if desired. Up to four additional colours can be added to give depth, but make sure you do not obliterate the base colour.

COLOURWASHING

This gives a natural, almost transparent, look to walls and is relatively easy to do. You can either buy a ready-made glaze for the top coat or create your own. There is no set rule as to which tools to use – a roller, brush or a cloth can give equally good results. Apply the base coat, using an eggshell finish if you intend adding an oil-based glaze on top. When the undercoat is dry, dip a brush into the topcoat and wipe off the excess with a cloth. Apply the paint in random, sweeping movements over an area of about 1sq m (11sq ft) at a time. The overall effect is meant to be uneven, so do not be too concerned by irregularities. Go over the whole wall with a dry paintbrush to soften the appearance.

USING A NATURAL SPONGE

1 Dip the sponge into the paint and scrape off any excess. Lightly dab on the paint.

2 Add more paint, continuing to work over the surface. Fill in any gaps.

SPONGING TWO LAYERS

1 Apply a single layer. When you apply two colours, the second layer softens the effect. Allow the surface to dry completely.

2 Wash the sponge out. Dip it into the second colour paint. Do not over apply it as the first layer must not be totally covered.

1 Mix the paint using 50 per cent emulsion (latex) paint and 50 per cent wallpaper paste (premixed to a thin solution).

2 Continue painting over the whole surface. When the first layer is completely dry, repeat step 1 using a second colour of paint.

3 Add more paint and soften the joins. The overall colourwash effect will be much softer than when using just one colour.

STENCILLING

This does not require a great deal of specialist equipment; many of the items used are commonly found in most households, but it is worth investing in a good stencil brush. The ends of the brush should be flat and the bristles firm.

If you buy ready-made stencils, most of the hard work is done. However, it's fun to make your own stencils, and useful too, should you need to make a copy of a pre-cut one that is wearing out. You can apply the paint with a brush or sponge. Proper stencil brushes have short, stiff bristles and are used with a dabbing action rather than a brushing motion, ensuring that the paint does not creep under the edge of the stencil.

To apply the stencil, draw a pencilled guideline at the midpoint of the wall. Place the stencil on this and secure it with masking tape. Pour a small amount of paint into a saucer or shallow tray. If using a sponge, moisten it with water, then squeeze it almost dry. Lightly coat the sponge with paint, then wipe off the excess.

Start painting at the outside of the image with either the sponge or a stencil brush and work toward the centre, dabbing the paint on with light, even touches. It is better to build up the colour gradually than to use too much paint initially. Gently lift one corner of the stencil to monitor your progress.

When you have completed the pattern, carefully remove the stencil and reposition it to your left or right. Continue in this way until you have completed the stencilled pattern. Wait for the paint to dry before adding subsequent colours.

TRANSFERRING A STENCIL TEMPLATE

1 Place a piece of tracing paper over the design and draw over it with a hard pencil.

2 Turn over the tracing paper, and on the back rub over the lines with a soft pencil.

3 Turn the paper back to the right side. Carefully draw over the original lines using a hard pencil.

4 Place the stencil on to a cutting mat or piece of thick cardboard and tape in place. Use a craft knife or scalpel to cut it out.

Ragging, Dragging and Stamping

Many paint effects require the minimum of tools and special equipment. To try ragging techniques, you simply need a clean rag and a choice of water- or oil-based paints. Beginners should start with ragging on, ragging off and stamping, before progressing to the more challenging techniques of rag rolling and dragging, as confidence grows.

Ragging

There are three different ways of creating an attractive mottled effect with rags: ragging on, ragging off and rag rolling. Each is fairly easy to do, but the last requires steady hands to achieve the best results. A light base colour with a deeper shade of paint on top is a popular choice for these methods. You can use an eggshell base topped by a glaze, or emulsion (latex) paints for both base and top coat.

Ragging on

Paint on your chosen base coat and let it dry. Mix 50 per cent emulsion paint with 50 per cent water or wallpaper paste in a paint kettle (pot) or pour a small amount of the top coat into a paint tray. Scrunch up a rag or chamois, dip it into the paint and dab off any excess on the side of the tray, then apply to the wall with a light dabbing motion.

Using the Ragging on Technique

1 Pour your choice of paint into a roller tray. Scrunch up a rag, dip it into the paint, wipe off any excess and dab the rag on to the wall.

2 Continue rescrunching the rag and dabbing it on to the wall until the wall has an even cover of paint.

Ragging off

You may need disposable gloves for this method, as it can be messy. Apply a base coat and allow to dry, then paint on the top coat; if using emulsion, thin it with water.

Crumple up a clean rag – cotton works best – and press firmly on to the wet top coat to remove some of the colour and expose traces of the base. Open out the cloth and scrunch it up again to vary the pattern. When the rag becomes saturated with paint, change it for a new one. Paint-soaked rags are highly flammable so allow to dry before discarding them.

Rag rolling

Allow the base coat to dry – an eggshell finish works well. Roll a lint-free cotton rag into a sausage

Using the Ragging off Technique

1 Mix 50 per cent emulsion (latex) with 50 per cent water or wallpaper paste (premixed to a thin solution) in a paint kettle (pot). Brush the wash on over a large area.

2 Take a rag or chamois, scrunch it up into a ball and dab on to the wall to gently remove small areas of paint. Vary the angles with each dab.

3 Continue working over the surface until the entire effect is even. If you are taking off too much paint, apply more with a brush and then dab the chamois over the surface again.

shape, then dip it into a glaze mixture and squeeze out the excess. Starting at the bottom of the wall, roll the rag upward in a straight line. Reshape the rag if you want to vary the pattern. Dip it into the glaze again, hold the rag so that it overlaps the completed section slightly and repeat the process.

Dragging

This effect works best on very smooth surfaces, as it will highlight every bump. Beginners should practise on a small area first to perfect the technique. An oil-based top coat, such as scumble glaze, will remain workable for longer than emulsion and is the best medium to use if this technique is new to you.

You can buy a ready-made glaze or mix your own. For the latter, simply mix one part glaze with two parts white spirit (paint thinner), adding colour with a little artists' oil paint. It may be difficult to duplicate the exact colour again, so make a generous batch to ensure that you have enough to finish the job.

Paint on an eggshell base coat and leave to dry. Then apply a line of glaze, about 600mm (2ft) wide, along the length of the wall. Begin at the top of the wall and drag a long-bristled brush down through the glaze to create a narrow, striped effect. Wipe the brush clean, then repeat the procedure until you have completed the wall.

Stamping

This technique is quick, easy, fun and an effective way of repeating a design on a wide variety of surfaces, using many different mixtures of paint and inks. There are lots of motifs to choose from, usually mounted on wooden blocks, and the effect has endless design permutations. Stamps are easy to make yourself from foam or sponge. Practise on paper before progressing to more ambitious projects.

You can use a black or coloured paint pad, or decant a little paint into a shallow tray. If using the latter, coat a mini-roller lightly with paint and roll it over your stamp.

Apply the stamp with a firm hand, holding it in place for a few seconds before removing. Repeat the process for every fresh imprint.

Cutting a stamp

1 Draw the design straight on to a low-density sponge using a marker pen.

2 Cut out the shape with sharp scissors and cut away the unwanted background areas.

3 Apply a small amount of paint using a sponge roller until you have an even covering.

Dragging

1 Apply the base coat and leave to dry. Mix emulsion (latex) paint with 50 per cent wallpaper paste or water. Apply the glaze in lengths, working on a small section at a time.

2 Dampen the dragging brush with the glaze before use. Take the brush in one hand and flatten the bristles out with your other hand. Pull the paintbrush down in a straight motion.

Practical tips

• Try the dragging technique on door edges to give a grained effect.

• Keep a rubber stamp clean for sharp images. Wash it in water or solvent depending on the type of paint used.

• When changing your ragging cloth, choose a near identical one to produce a uniform effect.

Preparing Woodwork for Paint

The secret of a good painted or varnished finish on wood is to spend time preparing the surface before you get down to the job itself. Wood must be sound and blemish-free, and any knots, common in softwoods such as pine, will need treating with a knotting solution (shellac) to prevent resin from seeping out and ruining the finish.

Pre-painted wood

If the existing paintwork is sound, there is no need to strip it back to bare wood. Simply wash the area carefully with a sugar soap (all-purpose cleaner) and water solution, lightly sand with abrasive paper, then remove any traces of dust before painting. Where there are patches of bare wood, apply primer, then undercoat as normal. Finally, you should sand lightly before painting on the top coat.

However, if the paint or varnish is chipped or blistered, you will have to remove it. Use a scraper to get rid of loose fragments; a triangular scraper, known as a shavehook, is handy for getting into tight corners and mouldings.

For stripping large areas of wood, the choice is between a chemical stripper and a hot-air gun. If you opt for the former, you will need to neutralize the surface, as recommended by the manufacturer, once the old paint has been removed. A hot-air gun will make light work of removing large areas of paint, but take care around windows, as the heat may damage the glass.

If you plan to paint over a faded woodstain, you will not be able to remove the old finish. In this case, simply sand the area, remove the surface dust, then apply one or two coats of an aluminium-based primer before over-painting.

If knots are showing through the painted woodwork, sand the paint film back to the bare wood and apply a knotting solution (shellac) to the knot, then prime and undercoat to bring the new paint film level with the surrounding paintwork. Sand between coats. Knots in bare wood should always be treated with a knotting solution.

Bare wood

There is a three-step sequence to painting bare wood:

• First, coat with a primer and lightly sand when dry. Wipe the surface with a lint-free cloth and white spirit (paint thinner).

• Apply an undercoat as specified by the manufacturer of the top coat you'll be using, and sand again. Remove any traces of dust with a lint-free cloth moistened with white spirit.

• Paint on the top coat. Normally, this will be a gloss finish, as it is hardwearing and easy to maintain. When varnishing bare wood, sand away any rough edges, wipe off the dust, then apply the finish.

Using liquid stripper

1 Wearing gloves, brush the stripper on to the painted surface. Leave it until the paint starts to bubble, following the instructions.

2 Scrape off the peeling layers of paint with a paint scraper. Use a shavehook for more intricate mouldings.

3 Wash the surface with water, white spirit (paint thinner) or neutralizer, as recommended by the manufacturer.

USING A HEAT GUN

1 Move the heat gun over the surface so that the air stream heats and softens the paint evenly. Scrape off the paint as you work.

2 Be careful not to scorch the wood. Use a shavehook to scrape out the paint from intricate mouldings.

3 Rub off any remaining traces of paint with wire (steel) wool, soaked in white spirit. Work in the direction of the grain of the wood.

FILLING DEFECTS IN WOOD

1 Fill splits and dents in wood using all-purpose filler on painted surfaces, and tinted wood filler on new or stripped wood.

2 Use the corner of a filling knife or a finger to work the filler into recesses. Smooth off the excess before it dries.

3 When the filler or wood stopper has hardened, use abrasive paper wrapped around a block to sand the repair down flush.

PREPARING PAINTED WOODWORK

1 Use fine-grade abrasive paper to remove "nibs" from the paint surface and to key the paint film ready for repainting.

2 Wash the surface thoroughly with a solution of detergent and rinse with clean water so that no residue is left.

3 Use a clean cloth moistened with white spirit (paint thinner) to remove dust from recessed mouldings and corners.

PAINTING WINDOWS, DOORS AND STAIRS

Windows and doors are key elements in the appearance of a house exterior. Flaking or badly executed paintwork will deter potential buyers and generally create a poor impression. Planning can be just as important as the mechanics of painting itself; discipline yourself to follow tried and tested painting techniques to ensure your home is presented to its best advantage.

THE CORRECT SEQUENCE

It is tempting simply to get on with a painting job to complete it quickly. However, there are logical sequences for painting windows and doors, which will streamline the process and give the best results. For instance, by following the illustrated guidelines for painting a panelled door, you will be joining a series of wet edges, allowing the paintwork to be blended completely before it dries. When using gloss paints, work with the grain and, since areas to be covered are typically small, aim to complete the job in one session.

ORDER OF PAINTING WINDOWS

When painting a casement window, keep the casements wide open as you work. Start with the glazing bars, followed by open casements, then paint the window frame last.

With sash windows, you will need to move the sections up and down to paint the various components. Paint the base of the top sash first,

LEFT The correct order of painting a casement window. It is best to keep the casements wide open while you work (see below).

PREPARING WINDOWS FOR PAINTING

1 Unscrew all old or existing window fittings, prior to painting.

2 Screw a woodscrew into one of the holes to make a temporary handle.

3 Carefully scrape off any traces of old paint.

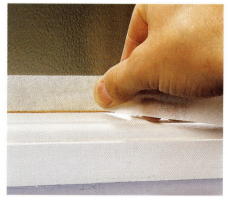

4 Apply masking tape, leaving a 1.5mm gap.

PRACTICAL TIPS

• Paint windows early in the day, so that they will be dry enough to secure firmly by night-time.

• Try painting the treads and risers of stairs in shades that tone with the general decor, or use a co-ordinating stencilled effect on stair risers and walls.

ABOVE Always remove door furniture.

ABOVE The correct order of painting a sash window.

then finish the rest of this section. Next concentrate on the bottom sash, and finish off with the outer framework – take care not to splash paint on to the sash cords; it will be very difficult to remove.

Order of painting doors

The order for painting a door will depend on its construction. There is one set of rules for flush doors and another for panelled doors – see the numbered illustrations on the right. Complete a flush door in one session, starting at the top left-hand corner and finishing at the bottom right of the door.

Order of painting stairs

For each stage, start at the top and work downward. Begin with the banisters and bottom rail, followed by the newel posts, top rail and handrail (if painted). If you are laying a stair runner and want a painted border either side of it, paint the edges of the treads and risers next. Allow the painted areas to run 50mm (2in) underneath each side of where the carpet will lie so no bare areas will be visible. Continue with the skirting (base) board and finally the side of the stairs.

ABOVE The order of painting a panel door.

ABOVE The order of painting a flush door.

LEFT The correct order of painting a staircase.

PREPARING EXTERIOR SURFACES

First impressions are of paramount importance, so the upkeep of the outside of your home should be at the top of your list of do-it-yourself priorities. As with interior decorating, time spent on essential preparation work will ensure the best possible result. It is best to start work at the top of the house and work down to the bottom.

GUTTERS AND DOWNPIPES

Clear away any rubbish that has built up and pour one or two buckets of water into the gutter to clean the system. Modern plastic gutters should require little additional preparation, but older cast-iron systems are prone to rusting, which can leave ugly deposits on brickwork and render. Remove the rust with a wire brush, before priming and painting. When it comes to repainting the walls, the rust stains should be treated with a metal primer, otherwise they will show through the new finish.

PAINTED WOODWORK

Exterior painted woodwork includes features such as fascias, soffits and bargeboards, as well as entire surfaces such as weatherboarding (siding).

New woodwork should be sanded lightly, working with the grain. Remove any dust, then wipe with a cloth moistened with white spirit

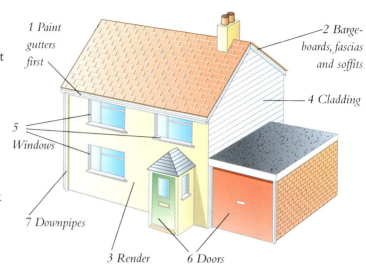

1 Paint gutters first

2 Bargeboards, fascias and soffits

4 Cladding

5 Windows

7 Downpipes

3 Render

6 Doors

LEFT Preparation and painting order of a house exterior.

(paint thinner). Seal any knots with knotting solution (shellac), and fill holes or cracks. Existing paintwork should be washed down with a solution of sugar soap (all-purpose cleaner) and water, sanded and wiped off with a cloth moistened in white spirit. Scrape off flaking paint and any bare areas should be primed and undercoated in the normal way.

For weatherboard surfaces, wash down with a solution of sugar soap, using a hose and car-wash brush

attachment to get up high. Leave to dry for a week. Replace any severely damaged sections and fill smaller cracks with a sealant (caulking). Punch in any protruding nails and cover with metal primer. Then prepare as for other woodwork.

WALLS

Mould growth is a common problem on walls. Look out for small white, orange, yellow, green or black marks and tackle them immediately.

ABOVE Rust stains should be cleaned off, then primed with a metal primer.

CLEANING BRICK SURFACES

1 Hose masonry down with water or a bleach mixture to get rid of dirt, dust and mould.

2 Apply paint stripper to remove any unsightly paint spillages.

Apply an approved fungicide, or clean with a bleach solution in the ratio of four parts water to one part bleach. Leave the former for 24 hours, then wash off with clean water; bleach should be left for 48 hours before rinsing off.

Mould and fungal deposits are often signs of a more severe problem, usually damp. Check the condition of any damp-proof course, and look for leaky downpipes, defective rendering and problems with brickwork.

Persistent white patches, known as efflorescence, are easy to tackle. They occur on new masonry as it dries out and can be removed with a stiff brush. However, if efflorescence occurs on old masonry, it indicates an underlying damp problem, which must be tackled before any redecoration is attempted.

MASONRY SURFACES

A sound brick finish can be very attractive, so resist the temptation to obscure it with a coat of paint on a whim. Porous walls will need treating with a clear water repellent to prevent rainwater from seeping into them, but this may be the only treatment necessary.

RENDERING

If existing render is in poor condition, cosmetic repairs may be made with an exterior-grade filler, while tiny cracks will normally disappear with the application of masonry paint. Many do-it-yourself

ABOVE A Tyrolean finish rendering can be applied with a hired Tyrolean machine.

enthusiasts will also feel confident about tackling larger areas of damage with a mortar mix. However, rendering a large area or a complete wall will be beyond the ability of most, and professional help should be sought.

The one exception to this rule is the application of a Tyrolean finish, which is produced with a light cement mixture. This is sprayed on with a hand-cranked Tyrolean roughcast applicator, which can be hired. It is possible to control the texture of the finish by varying the distance between the applicator and the wall. Similarly, you can vary the angle of application to create different effects.

WINDOWS AND DOORS

Exterior windows and doors can be treated in much the same manner as other outdoor wood. Start by filling and sanding any cracks or holes in the wood. Bare wood should be primed and undercoated, while old or defective paintwork will need sanding before over-painting. If the existing paintwork is badly cracked or blistered, it should be stripped off completely and a new primer, undercoat and top coat applied.

PREPARING WINDOWS

1 Remove any old putty from a window frame with a hacking knife.

2 Apply a fresh layer and use a wet finger to smooth it into place.

3 Then smooth the putty with a putty knife, holding it at an angle, and remove the excess.

4 Use a hot air gun to strip off old paintwork. Be careful to avoid heating the glass.

PAINTING EXTERIOR WALLS AND GUTTERING

The best time to tackle exterior decorating is in early summer or autumn, when the weather is fine, but not too hot. Remember that this work will be on a much larger scale than an interior-decorating project, so allow plenty of time to complete it. You may have to spread it over several weekends or take a week or two off work.

WALLS

There is a wide range of paints available for painting walls. Choose from cement paints, supplied as a dry powder for mixing with water, rough- and smooth-textured masonry paints, exterior-grade emulsion (latex) paints and exterior-grade oil-based paints for weatherboarding (siding). Masonry paints can typically be used straight from the can, but if you are painting a porous surface with a water-based product it is advisable to dilute the first coat. Use a ratio of four parts paint to one part water.

Exterior paints come in a wide choice of colours, but exercise caution with some of the more flamboyant shades. White, cream, yellow, blue, green, soft pink and terracotta finishes, which blend into the background, are generally favoured by house buyers.

ABOVE A typical example of pebbledash rendering. A coat of paint can greatly improve its appearance.

PAINTING WALLS

ABOVE Apply smooth masonry paint using a brush with coarse bristles.

ABOVE Apply textured masonry paint in the same way.

ABOVE To protect downpipes from paint splashes tape a newspaper around them.

ABOVE Use a banister brush to paint coarse exterior wall finishes such as pebbledash.

ABOVE Choose a deep-pile roller for coarse surfaces and a medium one for others.

ABOVE For speed, use a spray gun. Mask off surfaces you do not want painting.

Doorstep paint is generally available in shades of red in either matt (flat) or gloss finishes.

When tackling large-scale paint jobs, it helps to break down the job into a series of modules. Aim to complete a sizeable section in one session: for example, an area defined by first-floor windows, stretching from one side of the building to the other. Work downward, using fixtures such as gutters, windows and door frames to dictate where you finish. Hard paint lines will not be noticeable in these areas when you start work again.

Use a banister brush to paint very coarse textures such as pebbledash. Apply the paint using circular strokes and work well into the surface. To ensure good coverage on a medium-textured finish, use a coarse-bristled paintbrush and apply the paint with a firm dabbing motion or use a medium roller. On smoothly rendered surfaces, a large brush or medium roller are ideal. For the best results, apply paint in vertical bands crossed by horizontal strokes.

USING SPRAY GUNS

This is one of the fastest ways to paint a wall, but it can be very messy. Always mask off areas you do not want painted and do not hold the gun too close to the wall: a gap of 225mm (9in) is generally recommended. Move the gun along the wall in vertical strips, and overlap each one by 100mm (4in) for a seamless finish.

PIPES AND GUTTERS

New plastic pipes and gutters do not generally need to be painted. Older systems may be discoloured, in which case a coat of paint will rejuvenate

PRACTICAL TIPS

• Paint splashes are as problematic outdoors as in. Protect all vulnerable areas with dust sheets (drop cloths).

• Given the large areas to be covered, it makes sense to use a substantial brush, either 100mm (4in) or 150mm (6in), for exterior decorating jobs.

• A long-handled roller will help reduce the amount of time you need to spend up a ladder.

them. Clean the surface with turpentine, then lightly sand and remove dust before applying paint. Metal pipes and gutters should be primed, then an undercoat and top coat applied. Begin at the top of the work area and work downward.

If the pipework and guttering have an existing bituminous paint finish, you will need to apply an aluminium primer before over-painting to prevent the old finish from bleeding through.

PAINTING PIPES

1 Start painting pipework from the top and work downward.

2 Use card to protect the wall behind when painting downpipes.

ABOVE Avoid painting brickwork, if possible. Simply protect with a clear waterproofer.

Painting Exterior Woodwork

A wealth of products has been developed for painting exterior woodwork. Never try to economize by using interior gloss paints outside, they will not cope with temperature extremes and will soon flake and split. Do not be afraid to experiment with bright colours on woodwork, but choose a finish that complements, rather than contrasts with, other houses in the neighbourhood.

Fascias, soffits, bargeboards and weatherboards

Choose a dry, calm day to paint and avoid working in direct sunlight, as the glare will prevent you from obtaining good, even coverage. Furthermore, if you are using a water-based (latex) paint, it will dry too rapidly, leaving hard edges.

Start by priming any bare areas, then apply an undercoat and finally one or two coats of gloss. With a standard gloss paint, begin by applying the paint vertically, and then use sideways strokes to blend it well. Work in the direction of the grain, blending in the wet edges for a uniform finish. If you are using a one-coat paint, apply the finish quite thickly in close, parallel strips and do not over-brush. For weatherboarding (siding), paint the undersides first, then the faces, working horizontally.

Windows

Bare wood should be primed and undercoated, while old or defective paintwork will need sanding before over-painting. If existing paint is

badly cracked or blistered, it should be stripped off completely and a new primer, undercoat and top coat applied. Exterior windows should be painted in sequence, broadly following the pattern for interior casement and sash window frames. However, when painting a sash window, start with the bottom sash, as opposed to the top in indoor work. Mask windows carefully

before starting work, or use a paint shield to protect the glass from splashes. Remember to let the paint extend a little way on to the glass to prevent rainwater from seeping into the frame.

Doors and fences

If you have an attractive hardwood door, think twice before covering it with several layers of paint. You may prefer to let the natural beauty of the wood show through by applying a stain or varnish.

Stains may be water-, oil- or spirit-based and are applied directly to the bare wood. Teak and Danish oils are also popular for hardwood doors. They give a waterproof, durable finish and enhance the natural look of the timber. Apply with a clean cloth or brush. The final

LEFT Paint bargeboards early on in your work schedule. By starting from the top and working down you ensure that any dislodged dirt or paint droplets only fall on unpainted surfaces.

New or stripped wood   *Primer to seal*   *Undercoat (one or two coats)*   *Gloss topcoat*

ABOVE The sequence for painting wood.

Painting a door

1 Remove old paintwork, then smooth the surface with a palm sander.

2 Apply a suitable primer and allow to dry completely before over-painting.

3 Apply one or two undercoats and lightly rub down with abrasive paper between coats.

4 Apply topcoat to mouldings and panelled areas first, then move on to cross rails.

5 Finally, replace the door furniture. The finished door should last for years; simply give the paintwork an occasional wipe-down to keep it in good order.

coat can be applied with a scouring pad or 000-grade wire (steel) wool. If you want a particularly hardwearing paint finish on an exterior door, consider a high-gloss enamel. With this type of product,

you will obtain the best results by applying paint sparingly.

For fences and outbuildings, there is a wide selection of exterior wood stains and paints in all shades. Many are water-based and plant-friendly,

while being tough enough to withstand the rigours of quite harsh climates. Special paints and stains have also been developed for decking with a greater resistance to scuffing and cracking.

Painting a weatherboard (siding)

1 It is easy to miss sections of exterior weatherboarding, paint the undersides first.

2 Paint the facing boards next, and finish off with the end grains.

ABOVE Fences and gates can be painted in all shades of bright colours.

WALLPAPER PREPARATION

Preparing surfaces for decorating can often take longer than actually papering them, but it is essential. Before you start work, clear the room of all movable items to ensure that you have plenty of workspace and put down protective dust sheets (drop cloths). For reaching ceilings and high walls, make sure that you have the appropriate access equipment.

REMOVING WALLPAPER

Ordinary wallpaper is not difficult to remove and requires only wetting and soaking for 10–15 minutes before stripping with a broad-bladed scraper. Adding wallpaper stripper or a few drops of dishwashing detergent to the water will help it to penetrate the paper. Wallpaper that has been over-painted or that has a washable finish needs scoring with the edge of a scraper before soaking, but hiring a steam stripper is the easiest method, and you are less likely to damage the plaster surface.

If walls are faced with plasterboard (gypsum board), take care not to saturate the surface or hold a steam stripper in place for too long. Dry-strippable papers can simply be peeled from the wall, leaving the backing paper in place. If this is still adhering well and remains intact, a new wallcovering can be hung over the top, but if it tears, the backing should also be removed.

STRIPPING OLD WALLPAPER

ABOVE Stubborn wallpaper will be easier to remove with a steam stripper.

ABOVE Vinyl wallcoverings can usually be stripped dry and will peel off the wall.

PREPARING SURFACES

Once all the old paper has been removed, walls should be washed thoroughly with a solution of sugar soap (all-purpose cleaner) to remove dust, grime and traces of old adhesive. Rinse and allow the surface to dry. Cracks and gaps should also be repaired, and any stains that remain after cleaning should be sealed. For settlement cracks between walls and the ceiling or woodwork, use a flexible decorators' filler, and seal stains with an aluminium primer or aerosol stain block.

New porous plaster and old walls that are dusty will require sealing. A PVA adhesive (white glue) solution of 1 part PVA to 5 parts water is ideal for sealing these surfaces and will act as a size before papering. A coat of size ensures good adhesion of the wallcovering and allows paper to be manoeuvred freely on the wall.

PREPARING WALLS

1 Use a sanding block to remove any remaining "nibs" of wallpaper.

2 Repair any cracks and seal persistent stains with a stain block.

3 A coat of size will make the wallpaper easier to hang.

ABOVE The correct sequence of work when hanging lining paper.

LINING PAPER

This helps to disguise surface blemishes and provides a good surface for decorating. It is usually hung horizontally so that the joints do not coincide with those of the decorative paper, but hanging vertical lengths will be easier in narrow alcoves and where there are wall fixtures such as pipes. On poor walls, two layers of lining paper may be necessary; the first layer is hung vertically, the second horizontally.

The basic paperhanging techniques shown on the following pages can also be used for lining paper, but it should be left to soak for only five minutes to become pliable. Treat each surface separately and trim the paper to fit into internal corners. Do not use a ceiling as a guideline assuming it is level; mark a horizontal guideline for the lower edge of the first length with a spirit level. If you are lining both walls and ceiling, start with the ceiling.

PRACTICAL TIPS

• Allow at least 24 hours for lining paper to dry out completely before hanging the final wallcovering.

• Lining paper may shrink as it dries. Fill small gaps between lengths with fine surface filler and sand smooth. In corners, use a bead of flexible filler and smooth with a wet finger.

HANGING LINING PAPER

1 Normally, lining paper is hung in horizontal lengths across each wall.

2 Lining paper can be hung vertically in narrow alcoves or behind pipework.

3 To line a ceiling, work across the longest dimension of the room.

CHOOSING WALLPAPER

Although not as popular as it was once, wallpaper still offers a wide range of patterns and colourways, from very traditional to the most modern designs. Choose with care, particularly if you are new to hanging wallpaper, as some will be much easier to hang than others. Check the manufacturer's guidelines before buying to determine the suitability of the paper.

BUYING WALLPAPER

When shopping for wallpaper, ask for a large sample of any design that catches your eye so you can examine it in the room that is to be decorated. Look at the samples in both natural and artificial light, near a window and in a dark corner, as some colours and patterns alter dramatically in different lights.

Test a sample for durability by moistening it under a tap. If it tears easily or the colours run when rubbed lightly, the paper could be difficult to hang and maintain. Avoid thin papers, particularly if you are an inexperienced decorator, as they are likely to tear when pasted and may be difficult to hang.

Never skimp on the number of rolls you buy, and check that the batch number on all rolls is the same, as there may be a slight colour variation between batches that may not be noticeable on the roll, but could become obvious after hanging. However, the batch system is not infallible, so check rolls again for a good colour match before cutting and hanging. It is also worth buying an extra roll. Many retailers offer a sale-or-return service.

CHOOSING A PATTERN

Take a critical look at the room you plan to decorate and make a note of any aspects that could make hanging wallpaper difficult. Uneven walls and awkward corners, for example, can make pattern matching particularly problematic, while some types of wallcovering will conceal a poor surface better than others.

Regular patterns, such as vertical stripes, checks and repetitive geometric designs, will emphasize walls that are out of true, whereas random florals and paint-effect papers will not encourage the eye to rest on any one point and, therefore, will help to disguise awkward angles. Trimming can also ruin the appearance of a large pattern, so in a room that has a sloping or uneven

ABOVE Check that the batch number on all rolls is exactly the same.

ceiling, or several windows, cabinets and doors, a design with a small pattern may be a better choice. If a poor surface is the problem, avoid thin or shiny wallpapers, which will highlight every blemish.

If you are not an experienced decorator, avoid complicated patterns, as any mismatching will be obvious; instead consider using one of the many easy-to-hang, freematch designs now available.

ABOVE A freematch wallpaper or one with a continuous pattern, such as stripes, will not need an allowance for pattern matching.

ABOVE A straight-match pattern has the same part of the pattern running down each side of the paper.

ABOVE An offset pattern has motifs staggered between drops, which must be taken into account when cutting and measuring.

ESTIMATING QUANTITIES

Standard wallpapers are sold in rolls that are approximately 10m x 530mm wide (33ft x 21in). Use the tables to calculate the number of rolls required for walls and ceilings, remembering to add ten per cent for waste, especially if the design has a large pattern repeat. Lining paper is usually 560mm (22in) wide and is available in standard 10m (33ft) and larger roll sizes. You can calculate the number of rolls required from the tables, but there is no need to add any extra for a pattern repeat. For walls, measure around the room and include all windows and doors in your calculation except very large picture windows and patio doors. It is easier to measure the perimeter of the floor to calculate the size of a ceiling.

Depending on where they were manufactured, you may find papers in non-standard sizes, so do check. Wallcoverings in the US vary in width and length but are usually available in rolls sized to cover specific areas.

ABOVE Measuring up for wallpaper.

CALCULATING THE NUMBER OF ROLLS NEEDED FOR A CEILING

MEASUREMENT AROUND ROOM	NUMBER OF ROLLS
10m (33ft)	2
11m (36ft)	2
12m (39ft)	2
13m (43ft)	3
14m (46ft)	3
15m (49ft)	4
16m (52ft)	4
17m (56ft)	4
18m (59ft)	5
19m (62ft)	5
20m (66ft)	5
21m (69ft)	6
22m (72ft)	7
23m (75ft)	7
24m (79ft)	8
25m (82ft)	8

CALCULATING THE NUMBER OF ROLLS NEEDED FOR WALLS

	HEIGHT OF ROOM FROM SKIRTING (BASE) BOARD							
	2–2.25m (6ft 7in– 7ft 5in)	2.25–2.5m (7ft 5in– 8ft 2in)	2.5–2.75m (8ft 2in– 9ft)	2.75–3m (9ft– 9ft 10in)	3–3.25m (9 ft 10in– 10 ft 8 in)	3.25–3.5 m (10ft 8in– 11ft 6in)	3.5–3.75m (11ft 6in– 12ft 4in)	3.75–4m (12ft 4in– 13ft 1in)
WALLS	**NUMBER OF ROLLS REQUIRED**							
10m (33ft)	5	5	6	6	7	7	8	8
11m (36ft)	5	6	7	7	8	8	9	9
12m (39ft)	6	6	7	8	8	9	9	10
13m (43ft)	6	7	8	8	9	10	10	10
14m (46ft)	7	7	8	9	10	10	11	11
15m (49ft)	7	8	9	9	10	11	12	12
16m (52ft)	8	8	9	10	11	11	12	13
17m (56ft)	8	9	10	10	11	12	13	14
18m (59ft)	9	9	10	11	12	13	14	15
19m (62ft)	9	10	11	12	13	14	15	16
20m (66ft)	9	10	11	12	13	14	15	16
21m (69ft)	10	11	12	13	14	15	16	17
22m (72ft)	10	11	13	14	15	16	17	18
23m (75ft)	11	12	13	14	15	17	18	19
24m (79ft)	11	12	14	15	16	17	18	20
25m (82ft)	12	13	14	15	17	18	19	20

Hanging the First Length

Wallpaper can be hung using one of three methods, depending on whether you are using a ready-pasted, paste-the-wall or traditional unpasted paper. However, the most important step with any paperhanging task is to prepare fully before cutting the paper by carefully measuring the lengths and allowing for pattern matching to avoid mistakes.

Preparing unpasted paper

Measure the height of the wall from the ceiling to the top of the skirting (base) board and add 100mm (4in) for trimming the top and bottom. Measure and cut the first drop to length. To ensure a square cut, lay the paper flush with the long edge of the table and use a straightedge to mark the cutting line.

If the ceiling is quite level, you can cut a number of lengths. Match the pattern of each length dry off the roll against the first cut length to avoid problems with pattern matching as the job progresses.

Use the paperhanger's brush to weigh one end down, and line up the edge of the paper with the edge of the pasting table, then apply a thin, even coat of paste brushing outward toward the edges.

Fold the ends of the pasted length in to the centre and leave it to soak, checking the manufacturer's guidelines for the exact length of time. Long lengths of paper should be lightly folded concertina-style.

Ready-pasted paper

To activate ready-pasted papers, fill a trough two-thirds with water and put it at the end of the pasting table. Roll a length of paper with the decorative face inside and immerse for the recommended soaking time. Draw it on to the pasting table patterned side down so that excess water can drain into the trough.

For paste-the-wall papers, apply a coat of paste to an area wider than the paper – it can be hung directly from the roll or using cut lengths.

Cutting, pasting and folding wallpaper

1 Measure carefully, allowing for pattern matching and cut the paper to length.

2 Brush an even coat of paste from the centre outwards.

3 Fold short lengths of wallpaper end to end so you can easily carry the paper.

4 Fold longer lengths of wallpaper concertina-style so they are manageable.

Ready-pasted paper

Fill a trough two-thirds full with cold water and put it at one end of the pasting table. Roll the paper with the decorative face inside and immerse for the recommended soaking time.

above Draw the paper over the paste table, pattern side down to drain water.

THE FIRST LENGTH

Use a plumbline and spirit level to mark a guideline on the wall near a corner. The distance from corner to guideline should be one roll width less 25mm (1in), and the first length should be hung so that you are working away from (and not into) the corner. In rooms with a dominant feature, centre the first length over the focal point and work outward in both directions.

Place the first length next to the guideline, then adjust the top so that there is 50mm (2in) of paper lapping on to the ceiling and slide the vertical edge into its final position.

Lightly brush out the top half of the paper, working downward to expel air bubbles and firmly push the top trimming allowance into the angle with the ceiling. Make sure that the vertical edge is aligned with the guideline then continue to work down the wall, brushing outwards from the centre of the length.

Crease the paper into the junction between wall and ceiling by running the blunt edge of the scissors along the paper, then gently peel back the paper and trim neatly to fit along the creaseline. Brush the trimmed edge firmly back into position.

Ease the bottom half of the paper away from the wall and smooth it into place. Make sure that it is aligned with the guideline, then crease the bottom edge of the paper into the skirting (base) board and trim to fit using scissors.

HANGING THE FIRST LENGTH

1 Place the length against the vertical guideline and position carefully.

2 Brush out the top half of the paper and push into the angle with the ceiling.

3 Use the blunt edge of the scissors to mark the cutting line.

4 Gently peel back the paper and trim along the crease line.

WALLPAPERING CORNERS

External and internal corners are unlikely to be completely square, so never try to hang a full width of wallpaper around them as it will not hang straight. Hanging two separate lengths of paper and overlapping them slightly in the corners will produce a far better result, although some small loss of pattern will be inevitable on walls that are not perfectly true.

EXTERNAL CORNERS

Hang the cut length as usual, matching the pattern down the full length, then lightly brush the paper around the corner. Do not apply too much pressure, as the paper could tear but make sure that there are no bubbles and the paper has adhered well along the edge of the corner.

Use scissors to make a release cut top and bottom where the wall meets the skirting (base) board and ceiling. This will allow the paper to be smoothed on to the wall on both sides of the corner and trimmed along skirting and ceiling. Using a craft knife, trim the length vertically to leave an overlap of about 25mm (1in) brushed around the corner. Discard the waste.

Cut another length and hang this to a vertical guideline on the second wall so that it overlaps the strip of paper brushed around the corner, with its edge about 12mm (½in) from the corner and the pattern matching as closely as possible.

To do this, you may need to hang the new length so that it overlaps the previous length substantially. The width of the pattern will determine how much the two lengths may have to be overlapped. Trim through both layers with a craft knife and remove the waste. Brush out, then trim to fit the top and bottom as normal.

PAPERING AN EXTERNAL CORNER

1 Brush the wallpaper smoothly around the external corner.

2 Make diagonal release cuts at the top and bottom, into the skirting and ceiling junctions.

3 Trim off the excess paper to leave an overlap of 25mm (1in).

4 Hang a new length so that it overlaps the turned paper and matches the pattern.

5 Trim through both layers of paper using a sharp craft knife.

6 Peel back the edges, remove the waste and brush into place.

1 Measure into the internal corner at the top, middle and bottom.

2 Cut a strip to fit from the next length, but do not discard the offcut.

3 Brush the overlap allowance on to the facing wall.

If the wall is not completely square, the pattern may not match exactly along the full drop where the two lengths cross over. This cannot be avoided and should be taken into account when planning the order of the work. Always aim for the overlap to be where it is least noticeable. On a chimney breast (fireplace projection), for example, the overlaps should be on the side walls, not the face.

4 Measure the offcut and mark a guideline on the wall with a plumb.

5 Hang the offcut, overlapping the strip turned around the corner.

INTERNAL CORNERS

Hang the last full-width length, then measure the distance from the edge of the paper into the corner, taking measurements from the top, centre and bottom of the wall. Add a 12mm (½in) overlap allowance to the widest measurement and cut a strip of this width from the next full length. Do not discard the offcut (scrap) – put it to one side for use later.

Hang the cut length, brushing the overlap allowance on to the adjacent wall. Make sure the paper is brushed firmly into the corner by dabbing the wallpaper with the tips of the brush bristles.

Measure the width of the offcut and use a plumbline to mark a vertical guideline on the adjacent wall that distance from the corner. If the internal corner is badly out of true, take measurements from the top, centre and bottom of the wall, and adjust the guideline for the offcut so that it will not overlap on to the previous wall.

Hang the offcut against the guideline, overlapping the strip of paper turned on to the wall. Although there will be a slight mismatch of the pattern, it should not be too noticeable. Trim the top and bottom of the length neatly with scissors.

PRACTICAL TIPS

• If an overlap allowance puckers in an internal corner, make small horizontal cuts in the paper so that it lies flat.

• Keep a tube of overlap adhesive handy to ensure that overlapping edges of vinyl wallcoverings adhere properly.

• Paper with a straight-match pattern can be difficult to align in an internal corner. Hold a spirit level horizontally across the corner to check that the design is level.

PAPERING AROUND DOORS AND WINDOWS

If you follow the correct sequence for hanging and trimming the lengths of wallpaper, you should be able to paper around doors and windows with little trouble, and any small mishaps around windows can often be disguised with window dressings. The techniques described here can be adapted to cope with a variety of situations.

DOORS

Mark out the walls in roll widths first so that you know exactly where each length falls. Thin strips beside a door or window will be difficult to hang and are likely to peel, so adjust the starting point if necessary.

Hang a full length so that it overlaps the architrave (trim), matching the pattern to the last length hung. Lightly brush the paper on to the wall where possible, and then use the bristle tips of the brush to press the paper into the top of the architrave.

Locate the external corner of the door frame and make a diagonal release cut into this point with scissors. As you cut toward the corner, press the paper against the wall to prevent it from tearing. Smooth the paper down the wall and brush the vertical overlap of paper into the edge of the architrave.

Make sure the paper does not separate from the previous length as you do this. Crease the paper against the architrave with the back of the scissors, then ease the paper away from the wall and cut along the creases, or trim with a craft knife held at a 45-degree angle to the wall. Trim the top of the door frame first, cutting inward from the outer edge of the architrave. Wipe the paste from woodwork and paper.

PAPERING AROUND A DOOR

1 Drape the paper over the frame and brush the paper into the top of the architrave (trim).

2 Make a diagonal cut into the external corner of the frame.

3 Brush the paper into the side of the architrave using the tips of the bristles.

4 Trim the paper flush with the architrave using a sharp craft knife.

PRACTICAL TIPS

• Lightly smooth pasted paper on to the wall before trimming so that it does not tear under its own weight when it is damp.

• The junction between wall and door frame is rarely even; trimming the paper so that it overlaps the frame slightly will create a much neater finish.

• If the sides of a reveal are uneven, trim overlapping paper to 50mm (2in) and make horizontal release cuts down the length so that it lies flat, then cut a separate strip to fit.

• Complete all cutting and trimming around doors and windows first, leaving the trimming at the top and bottom of each length to last.

1 Drape the paper over the reveal and cut into the corners of the reveal.

2 Cut along the top of the window sill and make diagonal release cuts around the sill.

3 Brush the remaining flap of wallpaper into the reveal and trim to fit.

4 Ease back the paper, and cut and fit a patch in the corner of the reveal.

5 Cut through both layers and remove the waste to create an unobtrusive butt join.

6 Hang short lengths above and below the window, matching the pattern.

WINDOWS

Hang the first length overlapping the window, matching the pattern to the last length hung. Smooth the paper on to the wall, then make horizontal cuts into the corners of the reveal – the first level with the top of the window sill, and the second level with the top of the reveal.

Locate the corners of the window sill and make diagonal release cuts toward these points so that the paper can be eased around the shape of the sill. Brush the paper below the sill on to the wall, and trim to fit. Brush the remaining flap of paper around the corner into the reveal and trim to fit against the window frame.

Make sure air bubbles are expelled, but do not apply too much pressure. If the overlap is not deep enough for the reveal, hang a narrow strip to fit, matching any pattern.

Cut an oversized patch to fit the head of the reveal, matching the pattern to the paper above the reveal. Make a release cut in the outer corner, then slip the pasted patch into place. Tuck the edges of the patch under the paper above and inside the reveal, and trim through both layers with a wavy stroke. Peel back the paper to remove the waste and brush down firmly – the joint should be almost invisible. Complete the rest of the window in the same

7 Cut lengths large enough to be brushed into the reveal at the top.

way, hanging short lengths above and below the reveal. Lengths above the window can be brushed into the reveal complete provided that it is not deep and the edge is square.

PAPERING STAIRWELLS

When working in stairwells, safety is the main priority. Access equipment suitable for use on stairs may be hired, but you can also construct your own safe work platform. The main problem with papering a stairwell is having to handle the extra-long lengths of wallpaper. Apply paste liberally, so the paper does not dry out while you hang it.

CONSTRUCTING A WORK PLATFORM

To construct a platform, you will need a sturdy stepladder, a straight ladder and a sturdy scaffold board that is long enough to reach between the two. If you need to bridge a gap of 1.5m (5ft) or more, two scaffold boards placed one on top of the other will be needed, and if the span is greater than 2.4m (8ft), the centre of the boards will require additional support, such as a combination ladder.

The planks should be tied securely to each ladder with stout rope. If the platform has to be erected over balustrading, make sure that the feet of the straight ladder are wedged firmly in place: a strip of wood screwed to one of the stairs is the safest method.

ORDER OF WORK

Hang the longest length first, and work upward from the foot of the stairs. If you prefer to work from the top of the stairs downward, plan the hanging sequence carefully before you begin. Mark off length widths from the junction of the well wall and head wall, so that the last length will require the minimum of trimming at the head wall.

Hang the top half of each length, but leave the rest of the folded length hanging while you move the work platform out of the way. Then smooth the lower half of each length into place.

When measuring lengths for a well wall, make sure that you allow for the gradient of the stairs – as a rough guide, add the depth of three stair

BELOW The order of papering for the head wall of a staircase. Note that the ends of the straight ladder have been padded. Adjust the access equipment before brushing the lower half of the wall.

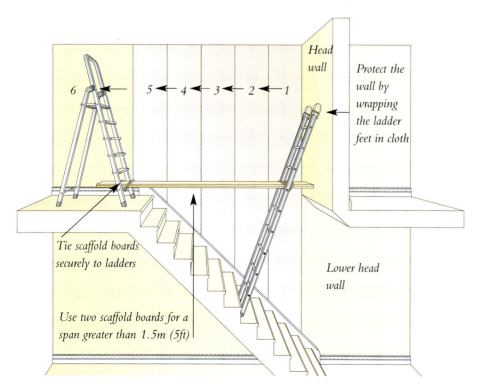

Head wall

Protect the wall by wrapping the ladder feet in cloth

Lower head wall

Tie scaffold boards securely to ladders

Use two scaffold boards for a span greater than 1.5m (5ft)

Well wall   Head wall

LEFT How to construct a platform for a straight staircase and order of papering for the well wall.

Make sure the foot of the ladder is secure

ABOVE The order of papering for the lower head wall of a staircase.

LEFT How to construct a work platform for a staircase with a landing.

risers to your measurement, as well as a trimming allowance.

Tackle the head wall next, hanging the top portions of the two or three drops needed, leaving the remainder of the folded lengths hanging. Adjust the work platform so that the planks rest on one of the stairs and are supported by a stepladder at the bottom of the stairs. Smooth the lower portions of the lengths on to the head wall from this new position, and trim neatly in line with the hallway ceiling. Finally, continue to hang lengths working along the lower head wall from the foot of the stairs.

HANDLING LONG LENGTHS

Unless your staircase is divided by a dado or decorative border, the drop from the ceiling to the floor will be considerable in places and the lengths of paper will be difficult to handle alone without tearing.

ABOVE Be especially careful to take accurate measurements. Mistakes can be costly when working with very long lengths.

ABOVE Hang the longest length first and work upward from the foot of the stairs. Hang the top half of each length first.

ABOVE When hanging long lengths, ask someone to help support the weight of the lengths of wallcovering while you hang the top portion.

Papering around Obstacles

Hanging wallpaper around any obstacle requires careful trimming to obtain a neat finish, and a sharp utility knife is essential. Make sure that the blade is kept free of paste, and renew it at regular intervals. Wherever possible, remove wall-mounted fittings such as lights, first turning off the electricity supply, as this will make it easier to achieve the professional finish you want.

Fireplaces

Hang a full length so that it drapes over the fireplace and match the pattern above the mantel shelf to the last length hung. Lightly brush the paper into the junction of the wall and shelf and trim. Cut inward from the outer corner of the mantel shelf, and support the rest of the length to prevent it from tearing.

Press the paper against the wall at the point where the corner of the shelf meets the wall, gently easing the paper around the contours with your fingers. Make a series of small cuts to allow the paper to lie flat, then use the tips of a paperhanger's brush to mould the paper into the precise shape. Trim each small flap of paper, then crease and trim the paper down the side of the fireplace and wipe any adhesive from the surface.

Radiators

If a radiator is too heavy to remove, turn it off and allow it to cool. Measure and make a note of the

Papering around a fireplace

1 Drape the paper over the mantel shelf and trim along the back edge.

2 Ease the paper around the contours of the mantel shelf by making small release cuts.

position of each wall bracket from the outer edges and top of the radiator, then hang the paper so that it drapes over the radiator. Match the pattern with the last length hung above it. Measure out the position of the wall bracket and make a pencil mark on the wallpaper at this point. Make a vertical slit with scissors from the bottom edge of the paper up to the mark, and use a radiator roller to feed and smooth the paper down on either side of the bracket.

Trim the paper neatly along the skirting (base) board and wipe off any adhesive left on the face of the wallpaper, skirting and radiator. Repeat for the other bracket.

Wall fixings

When removing wall fittings, mark the position of each screw hole with a matchstick (wooden match) and carefully press the tip through the pasted paper before it is smoothed into place.

Papering behind a radiator

1 Make a vertical cut from the bottom of the paper in line with the bracket.

2 Use a radiator roller to smooth paper down behind a radiator.

1 Trim away excess paper from the arch to leave a trimming allowance of 25mm (1in).

2 Make right-angled cuts to ease the paper around the curve of the arch.

3 Paper the inner face of the arch last, joining strips at the highest point.

ARCHES

Hang the paper so that it overlaps the arch, matching the pattern to the last length hung, then trim off the waste to within 25mm (1in) from the edge of the arch. Brush the trimming allowance on to the inner face of the arch, making right-angled cuts into the paper every 12mm (½in) around the curve of the arch so that it lays flat. Paper across the rest of the arch, length by length, using the same method of cutting to cope with the curved edge.

For the inner face, cut a strip of paper 35mm (1¼in) wider than the arch. If the paper has a definite pattern, use two strips with a butt joint at the highest point. Align the manufactured edge of the cut strip with one edge of the arch and trim the other edge with a knife once the paper is smoothed into place.

SOCKETS AND SWITCHES

Turn off the electricity supply and hang the paper over the fitting. Press it firmly against the faceplate, so that you can see a clear impression and make a pencil mark 6mm (¼in) in from each corner. Make diagonal cuts to each pencil mark with scissors, trimming off the flaps of paper 6mm (¼in) in from the outer edge of the faceplate.

Loosen the screws of the faceplate and ease it from the wall, then use a paperhanger's brush to gently push the paper behind the faceplate and wipe off any adhesive.

LIGHT FITTINGS

Turn off the electricity supply and remove the fitting. Bind the wires with electrical insulating tape. Hang the paper to the cable, mark its position on the paper and make a small incision. Feed the cable through the hole. Allow the paste to dry before replacing the fitting.

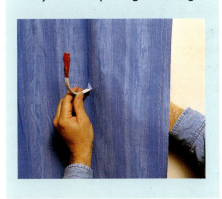

PAPERING AROUND A SWITCHPLATE

1 Turn off the electricity supply. Mark the corners on the paper overhanging the fitting.

2 Make four diagonal cuts from corner to corner of the faceplate. Loosen the screws.

3 Trim off the flaps of paper and push them under the edges of the loosened faceplate.

HANGING BORDERS

A decorative border can add the finishing touch to a wallpaper or paint scheme. You can choose from a wide variety of patterns, colourways and sizes, all of which are quick and easy to hang. The key to a professional-looking result is to make sure that the border is absolutely straight and hung against accurate guidelines, and that all the joins are neat.

BASIC TECHNIQUES

Use a spirit level to mark the position of the border on the walls at 300mm (12in) intervals, joining the pencil marks with a long straightedge. Measure from one corner of the wall to the other and add 50mm (2in) for trimming. Paste by brushing out from the centre, and fold concertina-style, leaving the paper to soak for ten minutes. Brush the back of a ready-pasted border with tepid water, rather than immersing it in a trough. A self-adhesive border needs to be re-rolled so that the decorative face is outwards.

To hang, place 300mm (12in) of the border against the guideline at a time, allowing the folds to drop out as you work. If using a self-adhesive border, peel away the backing paper and smooth it into place. Before cutting and hanging the next length, match the pattern on the roll. Do not attempt to hang a continuous length of border around an external or internal corner, instead use the

CREATING A BUTT JOIN

1 Form a butt join between two lengths of a border that has a simple pattern.

2 Use a seam roller to press edges and joins down firmly.

same technique as for hanging conventional paper.

If you have to use more than one length on a wall, a butt join can be used for borders with a simple repeat pattern. For more complex designs, overlap the two lengths so that the pattern matches exactly and carefully cut around a motif through both layers. When the waste paper has been removed and the cut edges smoothed into place, the join should be almost invisible. Use a seam roller to press down the edges.

PRACTICAL TIPS

• Hang a border by working from right to left if you are right-handed, and left to right if left-handed.

• Positioning a border is easier if the guideline is above a horizontal border, and on the inner edge around windows and doors.

• Fix a border below an uneven ceiling and paint the gap to match.

HANGING A CORNER BORDER

1 Draw a guideline for the border on the wall using a spirit level.

2 Fold a pasted border concertina-style so that it is ready to hang and easy to handle.

3 Match the pattern in a corner using a dry length, before cutting and pasting.

DIVIDING A WALL

1 Hang the two papers so that they overlap the pencil guideline.

2 Trim through both papers along the guideline and remove the waste.

3 Centre the border over the butt join and wipe away any traces of adhesive.

DIVIDING A WALL WITH A BORDER

A border will allow two different wallpaper patterns to be applied to a wall, one above and one below, by concealing the joint between them. Mark a guideline on the wall, approximately 900mm (3ft) from the floor, and hang a length of each design at the same time so that it overlaps the pencil line by 50mm (2in). Before hanging the next lengths, hold a long straightedge on the guideline and cut through both layers of paper with a knife. Remove the waste and smooth down the cut edges to form a neat butt joint.

When the room has been papered, the border can be hung. Centre it over the butt join using an overlap adhesive for vinyl wallcoverings.

AROUND A WINDOW OR DOOR

Draw a horizontal guideline to the full width of the border above the frame, and then mark a vertical guideline down each side. Cut the horizontal length 50mm (2in) longer than required and hang it, making sure that it overlaps the side guidelines evenly.

Add the vertical lengths, overlapping the horizontal strip squarely at the corners. Use the trimming allowance on the vertical lengths to adjust the border so that you will be cutting through the busiest part of the design. Holding a steel rule at a 45-degree angle, cut through both layers of paper from the external to internal corner of the border, using a craft knife. Peel back the cut edges and remove the waste paper from the wall. Brush the border back into place to create a neat mitred join at each corner.

CREATING AN INVISIBLE JOIN

Disguise a join in an ornate border by cutting around an intricate shape with a sharp knife.

MITRING A CORNER BORDER

1 Mark out horizontal and vertical guidelines using a spirit level.

2 Overlap strips and cut through both layers from corner to corner.

3 Remove the waste and smooth down cut edges to form a neat mitred join.

PAPERING CEILINGS

Wallpapering a ceiling is not as difficult as it may appear. The techniques used are the same as for walls and there are few obstacles or awkward angles to deal with. Although the job will be easier with two people, it is possible to achieve good results on your own. Adequate access equipment, however, is essential and will make the job very much easier.

HANGING THE FIRST LENGTH

Assemble your work platform across the main window of the room. Ceilings should be papered by hanging lengths across the room parallel to the window, working away from the light so that you are not in your own shadow and daylight will not emphasize the joins between lengths.

To mark a guideline for the first length, measure one roll width less 25mm (1in) out from each corner and drive in a nail at each point. Tie a taut, chalked line of string between the nails, then snap the string against the ceiling to create a guide for the first length. If hanging paper on a white ceiling, make sure you use coloured chalk to coat the string.

Cut the first strip of paper to length, allowing an extra 100mm (4in) for trimming, then paste and fold it accordion-style. Place one end so that about half of the trimming allowance laps on to the wall and the edge of the paper is aligned with the chalk line, then brush it firmly into place.

If you are papering around a bay window or alcove, make diagonal release cuts at the external corners to allow the paper to lay flat. Brush the paper into the side wall of the recess and trim to fit along the edge of the ceiling.

Once the first length of wallpaper is in position, crease and trim the long edge into the angle between the wall and ceiling first, followed by each end, using normal wallpapering techniques.

COMPLETING THE JOB

Hang subsequent lengths in the same manner, butt joining the long

PAPERING A CEILING

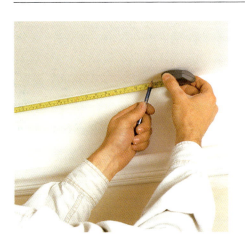

1 Measure out from each corner and mark the positions with nails.

2 Tie a chalked line of string between the nails and snap it against the ceiling.

3 Hang the first length against the chalk line, brushing it into place as you go.

4 Use the bristle tips to ease the paper into the angle between the wall and ceiling.

5 Crease and trim the long edge, then each end of the length.

edges. If there is a ceiling rose, turn off the electricity supply before brushing the paper over the casing and then locate its exact centre with your finger. Make a small cut in the paper at this point and gently pull the pendant through the cut, taking care not to tear the paper.

Ease the paper around the shape of the rose by making a series of small radial cuts from the centre of the rose to the edge of the casing. Smooth the paper into place on the ceiling around the rose and finish hanging the remaining paper. Crease the paper into the edge of the rose before restoring the electricity supply. The paper can be trimmed neatly with a knife once the paste has dried but turn the electricity supply off again before doing this. Where there is a large ceiling centrepiece, it is easier to hang and trim paper if a join runs through the middle of the rose.

Cut the last length roughly to the width required plus 25mm (1in) for trimming along the edge of the paper. Hang and trim it in the same manner as the first length.

ABOVE Paper into a bay window or an external corner by making a diagonal cut to ease the paper around the external angle.

ACCESS EQUIPMENT

Before tackling this job, it is important to consider how you plan to reach the ceiling safely. Access equipment will be needed that allows you to hang a full length across the room. Scaffold boards supported at either end by sturdy stepladders or trestles will create a flat, level walkway spanning the full width of the room, and can be adjusted to a working height to suit you. Use two boards tied together for a distance over 1.5m (5ft) and provide support in the centre.

PAPERING SLOPING CEILINGS

Plan the papering sequence so that a paper that has a definite pattern is centralized across the room. A sloping ceiling can be papered either to match the ceiling or the walls, but do not attempt to hang a single length down the sloping surface on to the wall below. Treat the wide angle between the two surfaces as an internal corner.

HANDLING PAPER

Long lengths of paper for a ceiling are easier to handle if they are supported with a spare roll of wallpaper or a cardboard tube.

ABOVE A spare roll of wallpaper can be used to support each length.

PAPERING AROUND A LIGHT FITTING

1 Turn off the electricity supply. Make a series of cuts into the edge of the ceiling rose.

2 Crease the paper around the edge of the rose, then trim neatly with a knife.

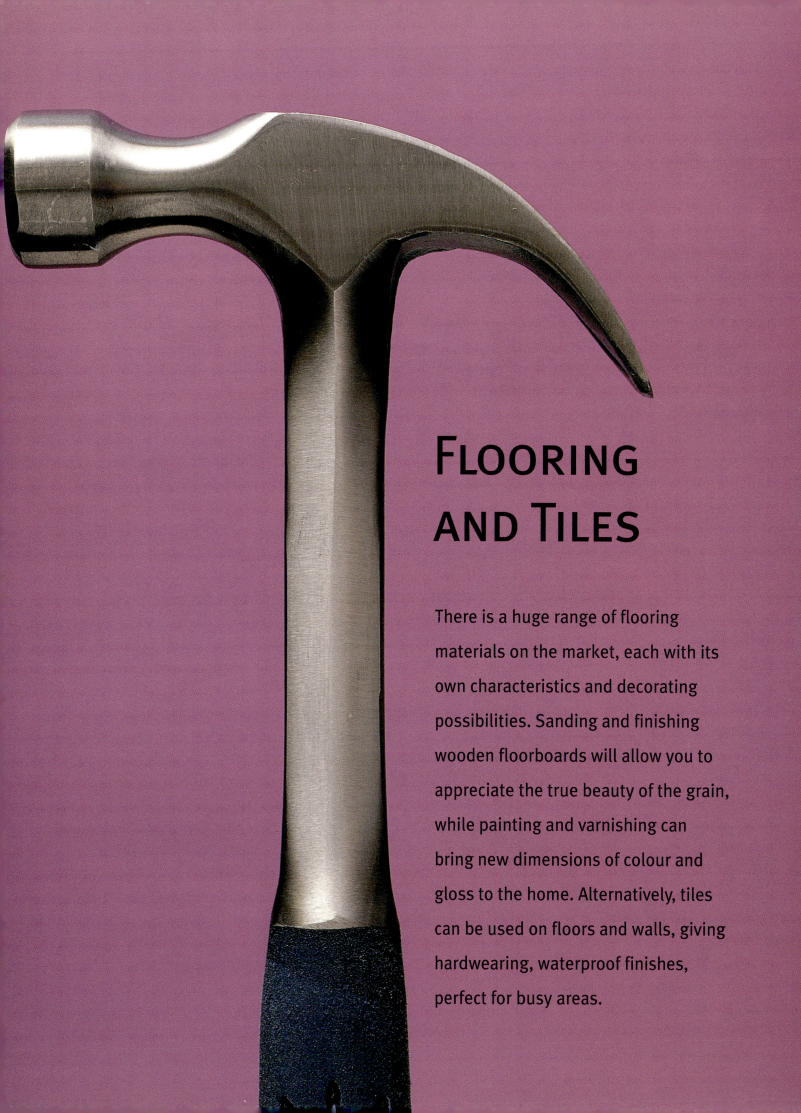

Flooring and Tiles

There is a huge range of flooring materials on the market, each with its own characteristics and decorating possibilities. Sanding and finishing wooden floorboards will allow you to appreciate the true beauty of the grain, while painting and varnishing can bring new dimensions of colour and gloss to the home. Alternatively, tiles can be used on floors and walls, giving hardwearing, waterproof finishes, perfect for busy areas.

Preparing Floors

Do not ignore the decorative potential of the floors in your home. There is a wide range of attractive materials from vinyl and cork to ceramic and parquet tiles, but all need laying on a sound, stable surface. Cheapest of all are the floorboards beneath your feet, which, sanded and sealed, can be decorated to suit your colour scheme.

BASIC REQUIREMENTS

The flooring is often the most expensive item in a room, so it must be laid and fitted correctly. All flooring requires a smooth, dry and level base, and a sub-floor will be needed over floorboards if sheet vinyl, parquet, or vinyl, cork, woodstrip, laminated or ceramic tiles are chosen.

Sheets of 3mm (⅛in) thick hardboard will be adequate for lightweight flooring such as cork and vinyl, but ceramic tiles will require a stronger base of plywood 6–12mm (¼–½in) thick. In bathrooms, it is worth paying the extra for marine ply, which offers greater resistance to damp.

Where flooring is to be laid directly on to floorboards, make sure that the surface is in good condition. Any protruding nails should be hammered in and loose floorboards secured with screws. A solid floor that is uneven or damaged should be repaired with a proprietary self-levelling compound.

ABOVE Punch any protruding floorboard nails below the surface of the wood to prevent them from damaging the new floorcovering.

LAYING A HARDBOARD SUB-FLOOR

1 To ensure a secure fixing for hardboard or plywood, use annular (spiral flooring) nails.

2 Condition the hardboard sheets by brushing or spraying with water before laying.

3 A piece of wood cut to size will allow you to space nails correctly and rapidly.

4 Use the offcut (scrap) from each row to start the next so that joins are staggered.

LAYING A SUB-FLOOR

Before laying, condition the boards by spraying the textured side of each sheet with 450ml (¾ pint) of water. Stack the sheets back-to-back flat, separated by strips of wood, on the floor of the room in which they are to be laid. Leave them for 48 hours.

Begin laying boards in the corner farthest from the door, fixing each sheet in place with 19mm (¾in) annular (spiral flooring) nails. Start to nail 12mm (½in) in from the skirting (base) board edge. To ensure the boards lay flat, work across the surface in a pyramid sequence, spacing the nails 150mm (6in) apart along the edges and 230mm (9in) apart in the middle.

Butt boards edge to edge to complete the first row, nailing the meeting edges first. Use the offcut from the first row to start the next row, and continue in this way, staggering the joins in each row.

ABOVE Nail across a hardboard sheet in a pyramid sequence to avoid creating bulges. Nails should be 150mm (6in) apart along the edges and 230mm (9in) apart in the middle.

ABOVE If there are plumbing pipes or electric cables under the floor, lay narrow strips of board over pipe runs to ensure easy access for future maintenance.

CALCULATING QUANTITIES

Before buying new floorcovering, take note of any aspects that could make laying difficult.

Sheet materials (carpet and vinyl)

Measure the length and width of the room at its widest points, taking the tape right into alcoves and to the halfway point under doors.

Multiply these two figures together to obtain the floor area, which will give you an idea of the amount of flooring needed. Draw up a rough sketch of the room showing all the dimensions and take it to your flooring retailer, who will calculate the quantity required and advise on how to minimize wastage and plan any necessary seams.

Small-unit flooring (tiles, slabs and panels)

Measure the room and multiply the width by the length to obtain the floor area. If the room has a bay or recesses either side of a chimney breast (fireplace projection), measure and calculate these areas separately and add to the total.

Hard floor tiles and slabs may be sold by the square metre or square yard. Purchase the quantity required plus a ten per cent allowance for wastage and breakages when cutting. Soft floor tiles and parquet panels are sold in packs. To work out the number of packs required, divide the floor area by the area that one pack will cover, rounding up to the next whole pack.

Strip flooring (woodstrip and laminated boarding)

Measure the room and obtain the floor area as discussed above.

Strip flooring is sold in packs to cover a given area. To calculate the quantity of packs required, multiply the length of the room by the width to give the area of the room and divide by the area that is covered by one pack, rounding up to the next complete pack if necessary. Different makes of woodstrip vary slightly, so follow the manufacturer's guidelines when laying the floor.

PRACTICAL TIPS

• Boards can be nailed in place quickly if you cut a length of wood to the correct length as a guide for spacing the nails.

• Lay hardboard with the textured side up. This provides a good key for adhesive, while nail heads will be concealed.

• In an irregularly shaped room, set out the stringlines and adjust the starting point so that any obvious pattern is centred in the main part of the room.

Sanding and Finishing Floorboards

A natural wooden floor will allow you to appreciate the true beauty of the wood grain and can transform a room. A few simple checks will soon tell you if the floorboards beneath your feet are worth renovating. While the work itself is quite straightforward, do not underestimate the amount of time that may be needed to complete the job.

Assessing the floor

A mechanical sander will not only get rid of ingrained dirt, polish and stains, but also remove deep blemishes and ridges between boards. However, the result will only be as good as the base material. Thin and splintering floorboards are not worth the effort of renovating, while a floor that consists of many sizes and types of board will not look attractive unless painted or disguised with dark stain.

Gaps, however, are quite easy to remedy: small gaps can be filled with a neutral-coloured wood filler, while large gaps should be plugged with fillets of wood planed level with the surface. If the problem is extensive, it will be easier simply to lift and re-lay the whole floor. Protruding nail heads and heavy deposits of old polish will tear and clog abrasive paper, and must be dealt with first.

Tools and equipment

Stripping a wooden floor can be hard work, so make sure that you have the right tools – hire those tools you do not own. You will need a drum sander for stripping the main part of the floor, an edge sander to reach right up to the skirting (base) boards as well as different grades of abrasive paper, a shave hook (triangular scraper) and a hand sanding block for getting right into tight corners.

A nail punch, hammer and screwdriver will be needed to knock in protruding nail heads and screw down loose boards.

above Sanding floors is a noisy, messy job. Protect your clothes and yourself with the right equipment.

Preparing the floor

1 Seal doors with masking tape to prevent dust from seeping into the rest of the house.

2 Screw down loose boards and punch down protruding nails.

3 Fill gaps between boards with a matching offcut (scrap) of wood or wood filler.

4 Remove traces of old polish with wire (steel) wool and white spirit (paint thinner).

Practical tips

• Using a sander creates dust, so wear a facemask and goggles.

• For safety, drape the electrical cable of a mechanical sander over your shoulder, and keep it behind you at all times. Use all power tools with a Residual Current Device.

Sanding

To remove the worst of the dirt, fit coarse sandpaper to the drum sander and work diagonally across the boards, overlapping each sanded strip by about 75mm (3in). If the boards are badly blemished or warped, vacuum to remove dust, then repeat this step, working diagonally in the opposite direction. Vacuum again, then fit medium-grade sandpaper to the machine and work up and down the boards along the grain, overlapping each strip as before.

Finally, repeat this step, after vacuuming, using fine sandpaper. Around the edges, use an edge sander along the grain, and finish corners with a shave hook and sanding block, or a disc sander.

If you are not careful, a floor sander can run away from you, and if used incorrectly it can spoil a floor. Therefore, it is important to know how to use it properly.

With a drum sander, tilt it back on its wheels, switch on and gently lower the belt on to the floor. Allow the machine to move forward slowly and do not try to hold it back or in one spot, or it will create grooves in the floor. Raise the machine back on to its wheels at the end of each pass, and do not be tempted to "spot sand" stubborn marks as you may end up with a deep groove.

Lay an edge sander on its side, switch on, lift it and lower it on to the floor. Keep the machine moving, otherwise it will create swirl marks.

Finishing and sealing

Once stripped and sanded, floorboards must be sealed with a flooring grade wax, oil, and polyurethane varnish or paint.

Wax is the most traditional treatment, although it attracts dust and is not particularly durable, so it is best used in low-wear areas. Brush-on liquid floor wax is the easiest to use, but must be applied in several thin coats, otherwise it will stay soft and look dull.

Floor oils are very easy to apply and form a hardwearing, water-resistant finish, but will darken the surface colour of the wood slightly. Rub with wire wool before the final coat. Follow the manufacturer's instructions for the best finish.

Sanding a wooden floor

1 Sand diagonally across the boards, using coarse sandpaper.

2 Use a medium-grade sandpaper, working along the grain. Finish with fine-grade paper.

3 Use a belt sander to tackle edges. Use a disc sander or sanding block for the corners.

4 Remove all traces of dust with a brush and then a damp sponge or cloth.

5 Sand down any remaining rough spots by hand with a sanding block.

6 Build a new protective finish with several thin coats of varnish, applied along the grain.

PAINTING AND VARNISHING WOODEN FLOORS

A wooden floor makes an attractive feature in itself, but it can take on a whole new dimension when you experiment with colourful paints, stains, waxes and varnishes. Bare floorboards in pristine condition cry out for innovative treatment. If you prefer traditional treatments, look at oak, mahogany, or beech stains coupled with varnish or a clear wax finish.

ESSENTIAL PREPARATION

Prepare the surface by vacuuming up all traces of dust, then clean the boards with a lint-free cloth moistened with white spirit (paint thinner). If the boards are already painted or varnished, the floor will need sanding. A hardboard floor will look more attractive with a painted finish. Use a primer first, then apply two coats of paint. Allow each to dry thoroughly, sand lightly and finish off with two coats of varnish.

The most important rule when treating a floor is not to paint yourself into a corner. Start at the corner farthest from the door, then work back toward the doorway so that you can make a safe exit while the floor dries.

LIMED BOARDS

Liming is an easy technique and a good one for beginners to try. It can be used in conjunction with colour-washing – the colourwash goes on first, then the liming paste – to produce an effect known as pickling.

Strip back any worn or grimy floorboards and apply a coat of shellac to seal the wood. Allow the

LIMING A WOODEN FLOOR

1 Stroke the floorboards with a wire brush, working gently in the direction of the grain.

2 Apply the liming paste with fine wire (steel) wool. Fill up the grain as you work.

3 Working on a small area at a time, rub the liming paste into the boards in a circular motion. Leave to dry thoroughly.

4 Remove the excess by rubbing in some clear paste wax with a soft cloth. Buff the surface with a soft cloth to give a dull sheen.

shellac to dry, then use a wire brush to expose the grains and provide a good surface for the liming paste.

For a very attractive finish, try using pastel shades such as pale green or blue for the background colour.

WOOD DYES

For modern schemes, consider colourful wood dyes. These must be applied to a clean, sound, grease-free surface. If the preparation is not thorough, the result will be patchy and unattractive. Wood dyes penetrate deep into timber, but they

do not provide a protective surface and must be sealed after application.

It is advisable to test the dye on a similar piece of wood before you start work on the floor as the dye will give varying results on different woods and can change significantly as fresh coats are applied. Finish the test with a coat of varnish.

If you are happy with the finish, apply the dye with a 100mm (4in) brush in the direction of the grain, working rapidly so that hard edges do not spoil the effect. Alternatively, you could use a soft cloth.

Wood stains

These do have a protective function and come in a wide choice of colours, in water- and solvent-based versions. The former dry more quickly, but this may not be an advantage when covering large areas, as patchy sections could develop. When staining a newly stripped floor, seal the surface with a thinned polyurethane varnish first.

Use a brush to apply up to three coats of stain, using the product sparingly and working with the grain. If, at some point in the future, you wish to over-paint a stained floor, you will need to strip the surface back to bare wood, then apply a primer and undercoat.

Floor paints

Specially formulated floor paints give a particularly durable finish, but in practice, many ordinary paints will suffice. The latter will need one or two coats of varnish to protect the surface.

Although paint will conceal the natural grain of the wood, it can produce an attractive, hardwearing

Applying a wood wash or stain

1 Pour the pre-mixed wash or stain into a paint kettle. Brush the wash or stain evenly on the wood in the direction of the grain.

2 While wet, wipe off any excess. This will even the effect and expose more of the grain. Leave to dry before varnishing, if required.

finish, which requires less preparation time as floors do not need to be stripped back to bare wood, although they must be clean and grease-free.

Varnishes

These are available in oil- and water-based versions, and in satin, gloss and matt (flat) finishes. Coloured varieties, a mixture of stain and varnish, give you the option of transforming pale floorboards into a rich spectrum of

colours, ranging from light honey pine to deep mahogany.

If you are applying a solvent-based product, ensure that the room is well ventilated. Stir the varnish well and use a wide brush to apply it. Apply a minimum of three coats. Rub the floor down with a fine abrasive paper before applying the final coat of varnish. On the minus side, varnish will crack with time. Every two or three years, you will need to sand the floor back to bare wood and treat the boards again.

Applying satinwood paint

1 Dilute satinwood paint with 50 per cent white spirit (paint thinner). Brush on the mixture in the direction of the grain.

2 While wet, wipe down with a cloth to remove the excess and even the effect. Leave the surface to dry before varnishing.

Practical tips

• Colours that work well in wood washes and stains include yellow ochre, blue, Indian red, violet, cream and pale green.

• If you use a solution of artist's oil paint and white spirit (paint thinner) to make up a thin wash, make sure you only use a small amount of oil paint, as the pigment produces intensely strong colours.

Laying Soft Floor Tiles

Soft floor tiles, such as vinyl, cork and carpet, are a practical and hardwearing choice for floors, especially for rooms such as the kitchen or bathroom. Not only are they quick and easy to lay, but they are also economical to use in irregularly shaped rooms. The look of the floor can also be varied according to the pattern in which the tiles are laid.

Vinyl and cork tiles

It is vital to achieve a symmetrical layout so that any pattern is centred in the room, and there is an even border of tiles around the edges. The first step is to find the centre of the room by joining the mid-points of opposite walls with lines of string pinned to the floor.

Working from the centre, lay a row of dry tiles along both lines of string until no more whole tiles can be laid. If the border tiles are less than a quarter of the width of a tile, adjust the stringline parallel to that edge of the wall by moving it over half a tile width. Make sure that the lines of string cross at right-angles, then rub

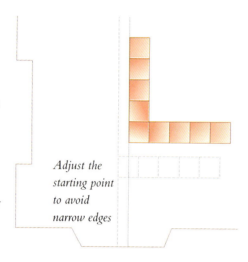

Adjust the starting point to avoid narrow edges

chalk on the strings and snap them firmly on the floor to leave a guideline in each direction. Use a notched spreader to apply adhesive to the floor, and place the first tile

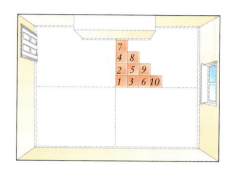

LEFT Lay two rows of dry tiles from the centre of the room and adjust the starting point.

ABOVE Complete a quarter of the floor at a time, laying tiles in the sequence shown.

accurately against the stringlines. To lay self-adhesive vinyl tiles, simply peel off the protective backing paper before placing in position. Work outward in both directions, laying

Laying cork tiles

1 Apply adhesive with a notched spreader to a small area at a time.

2 Lay the first tile accurately against the chalk lines at the centre-point.

3 Mark a border tile for cutting by using the edge of a spare tile as a guide.

4 For a corner tile, first mark one cutting line using the same method as for border tiles.

5 Swivel the tile around the corner and mark the second cutting line.

6 The L-shaped tile should fit neatly around the external corner.

tiles in the sequence shown. Butt cork tiles tightly together to prevent water from seeping between the joins, and wipe off any adhesive that oozes on to the face of the tile.

Complete a quarter of the floor at a time, starting in the section farthest from the door. Once all the whole tiles have been laid, leave the glue to set before laying the edge tiles.

To cut a border tile to size, start by placing the tile exactly on top of the last whole tile laid, then put another whole tile on top of this so that its edge butts against the skirting (base) board. Use the edge of the top tile as a guide for marking the cutting line on the tile below. The same method can be used to cut tiles to fit internal and external corners. Cut self-adhesive tiles to size before removing the backing paper.

At doorways, protect and neaten edges by fixing a binder bar across the centre of the threshold.

If cork does not have a factory finish, it will require sealing with flooring wax or at least three coats of polyurethane varnish.

CARPET TILES

These can be laid loose, but in busy areas, such as a child's room, secure the edges around doors and on every third row with double-sided flooring tape. Carpet tiles are usually laid in a traditional chequerboard pattern by alternating the pile direction; an arrow on the back of the tile shows the direction of the pile.

CUTTING TECHNIQUES

Cut vinyl tiles on scrap board, pressing the knife firmly through the decorative face. Cork should be scored through the face, then snapped

along this line. Cut carpet tiles through the backing material, holding the knife at a slight angle away from the pile to create a neat edge.

To cut tiles to fit around obstacles, first make a template. For pipes, slit the tile from the back edge to the position of the pipe, then cut out a circle for it. A piece of pipe with sharpened edges is useful for cutting neat holes in soft floor tiles.

SUB-BASES

Carpet tiles can be laid directly over floorboards, but vinyl and cork tiles will require a hardboard sub-floor. Soft floor tiles can also be laid directly on to a level, clean and dust-free solid floor, provided there is a damp-proof course.

CUTTING SOFT TILES

ABOVE Cut through the backing of carpet tiles with a sharp knife.

ABOVE Score cork tiles through the decorative face and snap cleanly.

ABOVE Make a template for curved cuts and awkward shapes.

ABOVE Cut a slit from the back edge of the tile to the position of a pipe.

Laying Hard Floor Tiles

Hard flooring, including ceramic and quarry tiles, stone and slate, creates a hardwearing, waterproof finish that is perfect for busy areas of the home. Laid correctly, it will give years of service. This flooring is not as easy to lay as soft floor tiles, so it is worth planning the layout first on graph paper and investing in the correct cutting tools.

Ceramic tiles

Plan the layout of ceramic tiles as for soft floor tiles, then fix two marker battens (furring strips) against the edges of the last whole tiles laid. Use a try or combination square to ensure the battens form a perfect right angle, and on a solid floor secure them with masonry nails.

Apply adhesive with a notched spreader to an area of about 1sq m (11sq ft), and lay the tiles according to the dry run. Use pieces of thick card or floor tile spacers to maintain even gaps for grouting. Lay up to a dozen tiles at a time, using a long straightedge and spirit level to check that the tiles are straight and the surface horizontal. Work across the room in this fashion, then leave the tiles for 24 hours to set before tackling edge tiles.

To mark an edge tile for cutting, follow the technique described for soft floor tiles. A proper floor tile jig will make cutting easier. Apply tile adhesive to the back of cut tiles, not the floor. Leave the floor for 24 hours, then grout it. Apply grout with a dry sponge to 1sq m (11sq ft) at a time, neatening joints with a grouting tool or piece of dowel. Wipe off excess grout with a damp sponge and, when it has set, buff the surface with a clean dry cloth.

Quarry tiles, stone and slate

Plan the layout and set out two guide battens in the same manner as described for ceramic floor tiles. The battens used should be twice the thickness of the flooring.

Dry-lay a batch of tiles and nail a third batten to the floor so that it butts against them and is parallel to one of the other battens. Check that the battens are level, adding packing pieces to adjust them if necessary.

Laying ceramic tiles

1 Mark the outer edges of the last whole tiles with two battens (furring strips).

2 Maintain even gaps between tiles with thick card or floor tile spacers.

3 Lay a batch of tiles at a time, then check that they are straight and level.

4 A proper floor tile jig is needed for making straight cuts in thick tiles.

5 Nibble away awkward cuts with tile nippers, piece by piece.

6 Apply adhesive to the backs of cut ceramic tiles, not the floor.

Mix mortar from one part cement and three parts builders' sand. Lay a 12mm (½in) thick bed for quarry tiles and 18mm (¾in) for stone and slate, levelling it by dragging a notched board across the bay. The cut notches at each end of the board should be the thickness of a tile less 3mm (⅛in).

Sprinkle dry cement over the mortar, then lay all the tiles to complete the bay. Insert floor tile spacers or pieces of dowel to maintain even gaps between machine-made quarry tiles. Use the point of a trowel to form 10mm (⅜in) gaps between hand-made tiles and slabs.

Tamp down the tiles with the unnotched side of the board until they are level with the battens, and wipe any mortar from the face of the tiles before it hardens.

Move the outer batten to form another bay of the same size and work section by section across the room until the main area of the floor is complete. Leave to set for one or two days. When the tiles can be walked on, remove the battens and fit the edge tiles. Apply mortar to the floor and level it first with a small notched piece of board.

Seal joints with a waterproof grout or point with a dry 1:3 mortar mix.

Cutting techniques

To cut ceramic and quarry tiles to fit around obstacles such as pipes and external corners, mark the cutting line on the tile and nibble away the waste with pincers. When most of the waste has been removed, smooth the rough edge with a tile file. Stone and slate must be chipped away with

a bolster chisel and hammer. For cutting ceramic floor tiles, hire or buy a floor tile jig capable of cutting thicknesses up to 18mm (¾in).

Sub-bases

Ceramic tiles can be laid on a plywood sub-floor over floorboards, but a suspended timber floor may not be strong enough for other types of hard flooring. Solid floors provide an ideal base, and hard flooring can be laid where there is underfloor heating or no damp-proof course.

Practical tip

• Tiles with a smooth back can be laid on a thin 3mm (⅛in) bed of adhesive, but tiles with studs will need a 6–12mm (¼–½in) bed.

Laying quarry tiles

1 Fix and level a third batten (furring strip) to construct a bay for the mortar.

2 Dry-lay tiles along the guide battens in both directions to check for fit.

3 Lay mortar between the battens and level with a notched board.

4 Use spacers or pieces of dowel to maintain even gaps between machine-made tiles.

5 Tamp down the surface with a length of wood to level the tiles.

6 Use a notched piece of board to level mortar for edge tiles.

Laying Sheet Flooring

A roll of sheet vinyl can be heavy and awkward to manoeuvre, but it is not too difficult to lay. The same method can also be used for laying carpet with a synthetic backing. Fitting fibre-backed carpet that needs underlay, however, requires a different technique and is a job best left to the professionals if you want to get the best results.

Planning

Sheet flooring allows a large area to be covered quickly and with the minimum of seams, but in an awkwardly shaped room can result in wastage. Plan the layout so that any joins do not run across or into a doorway. Seams laid at right angles to a window will be less noticeable.

Fitting

Unroll the flooring in the correct position, allowing the waste to lap up the skirting (base) boards. So that it will lay flat, cut away a triangle of material at each internal corner and make a release cut at each external corner. You will also need to make a series of small release cuts to allow the flooring to lay flat around awkward shapes such as door frames. Work around the room and trim away the surplus with a sharp craft knife, leaving 50–75mm (2–3in) lapping up the skirtings.

Start to fit the flooring along two straight adjacent walls, working out from this corner around the room. Use a bolster (stonecutter's) chisel to crease the flooring into the junction between skirting and floor. Then, holding it firm with a long metal

ABOVE To join vinyl, overlap the edges, align the pattern and cut through both layers.

straightedge, use a sharp craft knife to trim the flooring to fit neatly against the skirting.

If a join is necessary, carpet edges can be butted together – the pile will disguise minor irregularities. For vinyl, overlap the edges so that the pattern matches and cut through both layers with a sharp knife along a metal straightedge. Secure with double-sided flooring tape fixed to the floor directly beneath the join.

Once the flooring has been trimmed to fit, pull back the edges and fix double-sided tape to the floor all around the room. Remove the protective paper from the tape and press the cut edges of the flooring

Laying the vinyl

1 At internal corners, cut out triangles of flooring so that it will lay flat.

2 To ease flooring around an external corner, make diagonal release cuts.

3 Ease the flooring around door frames by making a series of small release cuts.

4 Trim away excess material, leaving an overlap of 50–75mm (2–3in).

5 Crease the flooring into the skirting, then trim using a metal straightedge as a guide.

firmly into place. Carpet laid over floorboards can be fixed with heavy-duty staples 18mm (¾in) in from the edge at 100mm (4in) intervals, or with 37mm (1½in) carpet tacks every 200mm (8in). When using tacks, cut the carpet slightly oversize, turn the edges under, and drive the tacks through the double thickness. Secure flooring in a doorway with a threshold strip fixed over the centre.

FITTING AROUND AWKWARD SHAPES

A profile gauge will be useful for marking out small shapes prior to cutting, but for a larger obstacle you will need to make a template. Tape sheets of thick paper or card to the floor, and use a small block of wood and a pencil to scribe the shape on to the template – this will be slightly larger than the size required. Lay the template on the flooring and use the wood block once more as a guide to transfer the cutting line on the flooring. Trim using a sharp knife and make a straight cut in from the back edge of the flooring to fit.

SUB-BASES

Carpet can be laid over floorboards, but sheet vinyl will require a hardboard sub-floor. Both materials

ABOVE Secure edges of vinyl flooring around the room with double-sided flooring tape.

can be laid on a level concrete floor that has a damp-proof membrane. Lining paper should be laid under synthetic-backed carpet to prevent dust from rising through floorboards and the carpet from sticking to solid floors.

LAYING PAPER UNDERLAY

Roll up the carpet half-way across the room and start to lay the paper underlay 50mm (2in) from the skirting. Work toward the centre of the room, overlapping each strip by 25mm (1in), and staple the paper to the floorboards along the seams and around the edges – use flooring tape on a solid floor. When one half of the room is complete, roll the carpet back into place, then roll up the rest of the carpet to complete the other side of the room.

PRACTICAL TIPS

• Re-roll sheet vinyl so that the pattern is outermost, then lay it flat for 48 hours in the room in which it is to be laid. This will make it more pliable and easier to lay.

• In a bathroom, it will be easier to start along the wall where the handbasin or WC is installed.

• Dust and fluff impair the adhesion of double-sided tape, so do not remove its protective paper until all of the flooring has been trimmed to fit.

• A carpet should be laid with the pile running away from the main window to prevent uneven shading in daylight.

THRESHOLD STRIPS

Make sure that you buy the correct type of threshold strip. There are various types suitable for joining carpet to carpet, vinyl, cork, wood flooring and ceramics. Remove inward opening doors to make laying floorcovering easier.

ABOVE In a doorway, use a threshold strip to secure and protect the cut edge.

USING A TEMPLATE

1 Use a block of wood and a pencil to scribe the shape on to a paper template.

2 Transfer the shape on to the flooring using the block of wood as a guide.

LAYING WOODSTRIP FLOORING

Woodstrip flooring is suitable for use in most rooms of your home and requires only basic carpentry skills to lay. The method used will vary according to the system you buy. Some strips need to be secret nailed to the floorboards, while others are designed to be a floating floor and may be glued, clipped or simply slotted together.

EXPANSION GAPS

All woodstrip flooring requires an expansion gap around the edges of the room to allow the floor to expand and contract naturally. This can be achieved by removing and refitting the skirting (base) boards so that they cover the edge strips, or by filling the gap with cork strip or covering it with quadrant (base shoe) moulding, which are quicker and easier options. Floor laying kits that contain expansion-gap spacers are available. Laminated strip flooring can be laid in exactly the same manner as woodstrip flooring.

FITTING

Mark a guideline for the first run by snapping a chalked stringline 12mm (½in) away from, and parallel to, the longest or most convenient wall. Normally, woodstrip is laid lengthways in a room, or at right-angles to the floorboards.

Use a strip of wood or spacers to maintain the expansion gap and butt the grooved edge of the first strip

Pull bar from laminated flooring kit

Glue scraper　　　　　*Tapping block*

Spacers

Professional tapping bar

Professional pull bar

LAYING A WOODSTRIP FLOOR

1 To allow for an expansion gap, butt the first length against 12mm (½in) spacers.

2 Drive pins at a 45-degree angle through the tongue into the floor.

3 If adhesive is recommended, apply glue to both the tongue and groove.

6 To ensure that the floor is strong and stable, stagger the joints.

7 Use an offcut to mark the architrave (trim) for cutting to the correct size.

8 Cut strips to size with a tenon saw and discard the tongue portions.

tightly against it. Lay strips dry to complete the first run and, if necessary, cut a length to fit, marking it with the aid of a try square.

Once the first row has been aligned and is square with the wall, ease the boards apart and fix them in place according to the recommended method. For a glued floor, apply adhesive to both the tongue and groove of adjoining boards, wiping off any that oozes between the boards immediately. Boards held by clips should have them driven into adjacent lengths at 760mm (30in) intervals. If secret nailing is required, drive pins into the floor through the board tongues at a 45-degree angle, spacing them 200–250mm (8–10in) apart, up to 40mm (1½in) from each end.

To lay subsequent lengths, push the grooved edge of one strip on to the tongue of the strip laid previously, tapping it firmly with a hammer and protecting the edge from damage with an offcut (scrap). Lay the second and subsequent rows in this way, staggering the joints. An offcut longer than 300mm (12in) can be used to start the next row.

If a strip needs to be trimmed along its length to fit in the skirting, place it exactly over the last strip laid and put a spare board on top so that its tongue butts up to spacers against the skirting. Use the edge of the top board as a guide for marking the cutting line on the board below, and trim to size with a tenon saw. To ease the last strips into place, use a lever, or fitting tool if supplied, and

pull them tightly against the previous row. If the flooring has been fixed by secret nailing, secure the last pieces by nailing through the face of the wood, punching the nails below the surface and disguising them with wood filler. Leave the floor to settle for 24 hours, after which the spacers can be removed and the expansion gap filled with cork strip or covered with quadrant moulding pinned to the skirting. If the flooring does not have a factory finish, it should be sealed as soon as possible with flooring grade wax, finishing oil or polyurethane varnish.

Cutting techniques

Cutting wooden flooring to fit neatly around a door frame can be difficult. Instead, use an offcut as a guide to mark a horizontal cutting line around the bottom of the architrave (trim) and frame. Saw through the architrave along the line and remove the narrow portion of wood. The wood strip should slip neatly underneath.

Sub-bases

Woodstrip flooring does not need a hardboard sub-floor, but it may require a paper underlay or polyethylene vapour barrier, so check the manufacturer's installation instructions. Floating floors and direct-fix systems can be installed over floorboards. A floating floor is the best option for a solid floor.

4 Tap each strip into place, using an offcut (scrap) to protect the edge from damage.

5 To mark a cutting line, align strips carefully and use a straightedge as a guide.

9 The last strip will need to be levered into place to create a tight fit.

10 Remove the spacers and fit cork strip into the expansion gap.

Practical tip

• Doors may need trimming to fit over the new floor, so remove them before you start.

Laying Wood Mosaic Flooring

Wood mosaic or finger parquet flooring is the least expensive type of decorative wooden flooring, and may be veneered or hardwearing solid wood. It is also easy to lay and economical to use, particularly in awkwardly shaped rooms. Some finger parquet is supplied pre-finished, while other types may require sanding as well as sealing after being laid.

Fitting

To mark a guideline for the first row, add 12mm (½in) to the width of one panel and snap a chalked line of string on the floor that distance from the wall farthest from the door. Butt a 12mm (½in) strip of wood or spacers against the skirting (base) board to maintain the expansion gap. Apply adhesive to the floor with a notched spreader, covering an area equal to two or three panels.

Lay the panels one row at a time, against each other. Do not push panels together, as this will force adhesive on to the surface of the wood. Wipe away excess adhesive immediately. Use a straightedge and spirit level to check that each row is straight and horizontal before going on to the next. Level uneven panels by tapping them down with a softwood block and hammer.

Once all whole panels have been laid, cut others to fit around the edges of the room by using a spare panel to mark the cutting line. Butt the top panel up to the spacers against the skirting to allow for the expansion gap. When trimming panels to size, cut down through the decorative face with a tenon saw; apply adhesive to the back before fitting into place.

Attach quadrant (base shoe) moulding to the skirting with panel pins (brads) every 600mm (24in), or fill the expansion gap with cork strip. Punch pin heads below the surface and disguise with wood filler.

Once the adhesive has set, the surface can be sanded if necessary. Use an electric orbital sander, paying particular attention to any uneven joints. Vacuum thoroughly and wipe with white spirit (paint thinner) to remove all dust. Then seal according to the manufacturer's instructions.

Practical tips

• To reduce the risk of warping, remove the wrapping and leave the panels in the room in which they are to be used for seven days prior to laying so that they will acclimatize to humidity levels.

• Set out panels dry first, adjusting the starting point if you will be left with awkward gaps to fill.

• The grain on parquet runs in different directions, making sanding difficult. To minimize scratching, lightly sand at a 45-degree angle to the grain.

Laying wood mosaic flooring

1 Snap a chalked line on to the floor as a guideline for the first row of panels.

2 Mark the expansion gap, and apply glue to the floor with a notched spreader.

6 Cut the wood mosaic panels face upward, using a tenon saw.

7 Wood mosaic can be cut to fit or slotted underneath a door frame.

CUTTING TECHNIQUES

To cut parquet or wood mosaic flooring to fit around a door frame, you can remove part of the architrave (trim) by using an offcut as a guide to saw horizontally through the frame as for woodstrip flooring and slip it underneath, or use a profile gauge to transfer the exact shape on to the panel and cut it out with a fine hacksaw.

To accommodate a pipe, measure and mark the position of the pipe on the panel, then drill a hole slightly larger in diameter than the pipe at that position. Remove a strip of wood between the drilled hole and the edge of the panel so that it can be glued in place, then fit the strip into the gap behind the pipe.

SUB-BASES

Wood mosaic flooring must be laid on a clean, dry and level sub-floor. A self-levelling screed should be applied to uneven solid floors, while a hardboard sub-floor will be required over floorboards.

ABOVE Use a profile gauge to transfer the shape of small obstacles to panels.

3 Butt panels against each other by aligning the meeting edges first.

4 Work in rows across the room, laying whole panels first.

5 Make sure that you allow for the expansion gap when cutting panels for edges.

8 Fix moulding to the skirting (base) board, not the floor. Punch the pins below the surface.

9 Remove all dust by wiping the floor with a cloth moistened with white spirit (paint thinner).

10 For unsealed floors, apply two or three coats of varnish or floor sealer.

PREPARING WALLS FOR TILES

A clean, level surface is essential for all decorating jobs, but especially when tiling. If there is the smallest trace of old adhesive, grease or dust on the surface of the wall, tiles will not adhere properly. Similarly, any unevenness will ruin the alignment of the tiles, and mirror tiles fixed to an uneven surface will produce a distorted image.

LEVEL OF DIFFICULTY

Beginners may feel confident about painting and wallpapering, but fear that tiling is beyond their level of expertise. However, provided the groundwork is carried out thoroughly, the task is relatively straightforward. If you are completely new to tiling, do not be too ambitious. Do not order top-of-the-range ceramic tiles until you have mastered the basic skills.

PREPARATION

Start with a small, manageable area such as a splashback. Set out the tiles so that they are centred on the section you will be working on, and where there will be little tile cutting to do compared with a substantial portion of a wall or an area around a window. Adjust the boundaries of your work if necessary, so that you will only need whole tiles to finish off the job and do not have to cut border tiles.

Once you have succeeded with a simple project, progress to cutting tiles and fitting them around awkward angles. Do not attempt to tile on top of hardboard or chipboard as they do not provide a stable enough background.

PLANNING

The most important thing to do is to plan precisely where whole tiles will fall. On a flat, uninterrupted wall this is quite easy; simply find the centreline of the wall and plan the tiling to start from there. However, there will probably be obstacles such as window reveals, door openings and built-in furniture in the room, all competing to be the centre of attention. It is necessary to work out the best centre-point to begin work from and care must be taken to avoid having very thin cut tile borders and edges.

Careful setting out is essential to the success of any tiling job. The object is to obtain a balanced look

ABOVE Use a scraper to get rid of blistered paint. Fill in any dents or cracks.

ABOVE Absorbent surfaces should be primed with a PVA adhesive prior to tiling.

ABOVE Wash any paintwork with a solution of water and sugar soap (all-purpose cleaner).

ABOVE Use a coat of skimming plaster to smooth out blemishes before you begin.

ABOVE Score the surface of old tiles with a tile cutter to provide a key for the new ones.

1 Tap the broken tile with a hammer protected by a cloth.

2 Carefully chip out the broken tile using a cold chisel.

3 Remove old adhesive. Butter the back of the new tile and slot into place.

on each tiled surface, with the rows of tiles centred on the wall itself or on some prominent feature, much as you would centre a wallpaper pattern. This will ensure that any cut tiles at the margins or around a feature are of equal size. Doors and window openings particularly can cause problems and often require quite a bit of thought.

You will need to work quite quickly, as the adhesive and grout will begin to dry out rapidly. Tackle small sections at a time, cleaning off any excess as you go before it has a chance to harden. This is particularly important with combined adhesives and grouts.

PRACTICAL TIPS

• Never mix floor and wall tiles. The former will be too heavy to adhere to walls. Similarly, wall tiles are far too fragile to use on floors.

• Look for authentic, relief-pattern Victorian tiles to add a little luxury to your decor. Salvage yards and antique shops are a good source.

SURFACES

It is vital to prepare the surface to be tiled properly, so that the tiles will adhere well. The surface for tiling should be clean and dry. It is possible to tile over painted plaster or plasterboard (gypsum board), but old wall coverings should be removed and brick walls must be rendered.

Printed wallpaper can easily be removed because it will absorb water splashed on it immediately; other types will not. With paper-backed fabric wall coverings, it is often possible to peel the fabric away from its paper backing; try it before turning to other methods.

Modern tile adhesives allow tiling over existing tiles, so there is no need to remove these if they are even and securely bonded to the wall surface. Removing tiles might leave you with a time-consuming plastering job before you start. Score the surface of the tiles to provide a key for the adhesive.

Wash wall surfaces down with sugar soap (all-purpose cleaner) or detergent, working from the bottom up, then rinse them with clean water, working from the top down.

TILING CHECKLIST

• Never attempt to tile over old wallcoverings. Remove every scrap of paper and make sure that the wall behind is solid and stable. Remove any flaking plasterwork and repair any cracks.

• Allow new plaster to dry out completely before tiling, then apply a primer sealer to prevent the tile adhesive from soaking into the surface.

• It is possible to tile over existing tiles if they are fixed firmly, although generally it is preferable to remove them. Key the surface of the old tiles by rubbing them down with silicon-carbide paper, score and then wipe clean. Do not line up the old and new tiles. Aim to vary the pattern so that new grout lines are created.

• Painted walls should be washed down, lightly keyed with sandpaper, then all dust removed with a damp cloth.

PLANNING AND ESTIMATING

Successful tiling relies on good planning. Ceramic tiles, the most popular choice for tiling, can be very expensive, especially if you opt for ornate designs or hand-decorated types, and mistakes could prove very costly. Most tiles are produced in standard sizes, so it is a simple matter to work out exactly how many you need to complete a job.

HOW MANY TILES?

Our table lists one of the commonest tile sizes, 150 x 150mm (6 x 6in), but tiles come in a wide variety of shapes and sizes, ranging from tiny mosaics to large tiles measuring 400 x 300mm (15¾ x 11¾in) and over.

Begin by measuring the height and width of the space you want to tile, then multiply these figures to give you the overall area in square metres (or square yards). Then you need to establish how many of your chosen tiles will be needed to fill this space. Many manufacturers will specify the number of tiles required to cover a given area. This is invaluable if the tiles have a non-standard shape. Then it is a simple matter to work out the required number for the whole area. For example, if you need to cover a space of 10sq m (10sq yd) and there are 16 tiles to the square metre (square yard), you will need 160 tiles to complete the job. However, you should also allow an extra ten per cent for breakages, which would bring the total to 176.

ABOVE If your tile design is complex, for example, with motif tiles used sparingly in a run of expensive tiles, use graph paper to plan the final layout. Use a large square to represent each tile.

CERAMIC COVING TILES

These small ceramic tiles offer a neat alternative to plastic strip or waterproof sealants around areas such as shower trays and baths.

Bullnose tile

Use this to round off a run of coving tiles.

Quadrant

Neatly fills gaps around the bath.

Mitred tile

Mitred tiles give a neat finish to corners.

CALCULATING THE NUMBER OF TILES REQUIRED

Measure the height and width of the area to be tiled and use the chart to calculate how many tiles you will need.

APPROXIMATE NUMBER OF 15 X 15CM (6 X 6IN) TILES REQUIRED

	0.3m/1ft	0.61m/2ft	0.91m/3ft	1.21m/4ft	1.52m/5ft	1.82m/6ft	2.13m/7ft	2.43m/8ft	2.74m/9ft	3.05m/10ft	3.35m/11ft	3.65m/12ft
2.74m/9ft	36	72	108	144	180	216	252	288	324	360	396	432
2.43m/8ft	32	64	96	128	160	192	224	256	288	320	352	384
2.13m/7ft	28	56	84	112	140	168	196	224	252	280	308	336
1.82m/6ft	24	48	72	96	120	144	168	192	216	240	264	288
1.52m/5ft	20	40	60	80	100	120	140	160	180	200	220	240
1.21m/4ft	16	32	48	64	80	96	112	128	144	160	176	192
0.91m/3ft	12	24	36	48	60	72	84	96	108	120	132	144
0.61m/2ft	8	16	24	32	40	48	56	64	72	80	88	96
0.3m/1ft	4	8	12	16	20	24	28	32	36	40	44	48

Which tiles?

In general, the cheapest tiles are those with no pattern. However, a large area of a plain colour may look better if enlivened with patterned border tiles or a plaque, comprising a number of tiles that fit together to make a larger picture. Or, pretty motif tiles can be used sparingly on a predominantly plain wall to add colour and interest. Although ceramic tiles are the most popular choice, you could also use vitreous glass, mirror, metallic, mosaic, cork or terracotta tiles for your walls. Buy your tiles in bulk, making sure that any batch number is the same on each box as there can be significant differences in shading between batches. You can also disguise the differences in colour by mixing up all the tiles before you begin.

Tiling gauge

Make a tile gauge from a 50 x 25mm (2 x 1in) strip of wood, cut to about 2m (6ft 7in) long. Place it on the floor and lay your tiles along it. If you are using standard field tiles, allow room for the spacers, then mark the position of each tile on the gauge. Draw a line at the top of the horizontal tiling area and use a spirit level to ensure it is level.

Use your gauging rod vertically to mark off the tiles down the length of the wall. If you need to cut the tiles to fit, they will be much less noticeable at the bottom. Use masonry nails to secure a batten (furring strip) where the last full tiles will be positioned at the base of your work area. The batten acts as a guideline for your gauge and will also support your tiles.

ABOVE If you are tiling a small area, such as a splashback, plan the job so you can position a tile either side of the centre point.

Use a plumbline and mark a vertical line down the centre of your tiling area. Position your gauge rod to work out where the whole tiles will fall on each side of the line. Nail in a vertical batten to indicate where the final vertical row will fall. These two battens form the perimeter of your work.

Fitting support battens

1 Place the tile gauge on the floor. Mark the position of the tiles and spacers on the gauge.

2 Draw a line at the top of the tiling area and use the spirit level to check it is accurate.

3 Using your gauge, mark off the tiles down the length of the wall.

4 Secure the batten (furring strip) to the wall to act as a guide for your bottom row of tiles.

5 Use a plumbline to get a vertical line and mark with a pencil.

6 Nail in a vertical batten with masonry nails to show where the final row of tiles will fall.

Cutting Tiles

Although there are several very good devices to help you cut tiles successfully, you will achieve much better results if you carry out a few practice runs first. Experiment on old tiles or sacrifice a few plain tiles to perfect the technique. It may be worth investing in a tile jig to help you achieve professional results when cutting large quantities of tiles.

Professional results

Badly cut tiles with jagged edges will be an eyesore wherever they are placed. If you find it impossible to obtain consistently good results, approach your tile supplier, as many will be prepared to cut them for you, but make sure you mark them clearly and accurately. When fixing small pieces of tile, use a notched spreader to apply adhesive to the tile itself, rather than the wall. This should keep excess adhesive off adjoining tiles.

Scoring/cutting devices

Straight cuts are the simplest to make. For example, cutting a tile to fit into a corner or to fill the gap at the bottom of a run of whole tiles.

A tile-cutting jig or hand-held cutter will make light work of this, but the former may not be able to cope with diagonal cuts. In which case, a hand-held tool should be used, scoring along the cutting line and snapping the tile in two in the

Cutting techniques

1 To cut with a hand tool, mark the cutting line, then score along it.

2 Place the tile, face up, over a pencil. Gently press, as shown, to snap the tile in two.

3 Score and cut devices hold the tile in the jaws of the tool. First score along the line.

4 Apply pressure to lock the jaws of the tool on the tile and snap.

jaws of the tool or over two matches or a pencil.

For irregular and awkward shapes, around basins and pipes for example, you will need to make a template to

Cutting awkward shapes

1 When cutting narrow awkward shapes, use tile nippers to nibble away small amounts.

2 Smooth down any rough edges on cut tiles with a tile file.

transfer the shape to the tile. Alternatively, a profile gauge can be used to copy the shape. This incorporates a series of plastic fingers that reproduce the outline of the object you want to copy when you press them against it. Narrow sections of tile can be cut away piece by piece with tile nippers.

MIRROR TILES

To cut a mirror tile, place it, face-up, on a flat surface protected by a cloth or newspaper. Mark the cutting line with a straightedge, then run a glasscutter along the line in one smooth stroke.

Place the straightedge under the tile and use the handle of the glasscutter to tap the surface of the tile lightly along the line of the cut. This will ensure a clean break.

Finally, position the tile so that the scored line is aligned exactly with the straightedge. Protect the surface of the tile with newspaper, then place a hand on each side of the straightedge, pressing down firmly to snap it in two. Wear safety goggles when doing this. Alternatively, a local glass supplier will cut the tiles for you, and smooth down any rough edges, for a small fee.

CUTTING A CURVED SHAPE

1 Trace the shape of the tile on to paper or card. Use it to make a template of the obstacle.

2 Copy the outline of the obstacle on the tile with a chinagraph (wax) pencil.

3 Hold the tile firmly in a vice, then use a tile saw to cut out the circular shape.

4 Remove from the vice and smooth down any rough edges with a flexible tile file.

MOSAIC TILES

These are fixed to a mesh backing and are trimmed by cutting through the backing with scissors. Some may have a paper facing, which is also easily cut. Individual tiles can be cut with tile nippers.

CUTTING BORDER TILES

Each border tile should be marked and cut individually as walls can often be uneven and the dimensions may vary on a run of tiles. Once the tile is cut to size, file smooth any sharp edges.

TAKING MEASUREMENTS

1 Measure the space between the last full tile and the wall or floor.

2 Transfer this measurement to the tile, score and snap to size.

FITTING FIELD TILES

All tiling jobs begin by filling in the central area to be tiled with whole tiles, known as field tiles. These need positioning accurately and supporting on the wall while the adhesive dries, otherwise they will slip under their own weight. Nailing vertical and horizontal wooden battens (furring strips) temporarily to the wall will provide this support.

ADHESIVE

Choose the adhesive carefully, making sure you buy a waterproof version for wet areas, such as for shower cubicles and baths. If you opt for a combined adhesive and grout, wipe any excess from the face of the tiles immediately; once dry, it will be very difficult to remove.

BEGINNING TO TILE

Spread on tile adhesive with a spreader or pointing trowel, to a depth of about 3mm (⅛in), covering an area of approximately 1sq m (11sq ft). Then, holding a notched or serrated spreader at an angle of about 45 degrees, pull it across the wall to form even ridges of adhesive. This will provide the best adhesion. Start at the bottom of the work area, in the angle created by the two guide battens (furring strips), and press the first tile firmly in place.

Position the second tile, using tile spacers to ensure a consistent gap if you are using standard field tiles. Simply butt universal tiles together.

Carry on until you complete the first row, then start on the next row, working from the edge batten as before. As you work, adjust the tiles to ensure that they are all bedded to the same depth. If any are proud of the surface, apply extra pressure to ease them into place.

Any tile that is slightly out of line should be removed immediately and repositioned; a misplaced tile can ruin the appearance of the entire job. If you have put too much adhesive on the wall, remove it

FITTING THE TILES

1 Spread a layer of tile adhesive with a spreader over an area of 1sq m (11sq ft).

2 Start at the bottom of the work area, in the corner where the two guide battens meet.

3 Position the second tile, using tile spacers to create an even gap with standard field tiles.

4 Complete the first row, then position the next row in line with the batten as before.

5 If you get too much adhesive on the wall at the top of the tiling, remove it with a knife.

6 Continue until the wall is complete. Allow the adhesive to dry and remove the battens.

carefully with a stripping knife. Wipe any adhesive from the face of the tiles with a damp sponge. Continue in this way until all the whole tiles have been applied. Allow at least a day for the adhesive to dry, then remove the support battens, taking care not to damage the tiles. Finally, cut tiles to fit around the edges.

CUT TILES

These often leave a slightly jagged edge which can be smoothed off with a tile file. You can fix the tile in the jaws of a vice or hold it in your hand. If using a vice, use a cloth to protect the decorative face from being scratched by the jaws of the vice. Hold the tile at an angle of about 45 degrees. File only in one direction with the glazed, decorative surface uppermost. Pull the file downwards without great pressure; repeat until the edge is smooth. If needed, you can finish off with abrasive paper wrapped around a wood or cork block.

TILING AROUND PIPEWORK

Inevitably, you will encounter a pipe projecting from a wall. This cannot be avoided. Assuming that the pipe will pass approximately through the centre of the tile, make a cardboard template, in two halves, and when the fit is perfect, transfer the position of the pipe to the tile using a chinagraph (wax) pencil.

Next, draw a cutting line to pass directly through the outline of the hole. Using whatever cutting method you prefer, cut the tile. Clamp each half of the tile in a vice and saw out the semi-circle in each tile. Use a tile file to smooth the edges then fit the two halves on the wall. If the work is done carefully, the joint line will barely be visible.

MOSAIC TILES

You can use sheets of mosaic tiles to make a feature among full-sized tiles, as a splashback or to cover an entire wall. Alternatively, you can create an attractive border or dado (chair) rail effect. Individual tiles can be used to create unique patterns on a wide range of surfaces.

If the sheet of mosaic has a net, mesh or nylon backing, apply adhesive directly to the wall in the normal way, then press the sheet carefully into place. Bed the sheets in place by using a mallet to tap

lightly against a rectangle of wood covered with carpet. This will soften the impact of the blow and protect the tiles from damage. The space between the tiles is determined by the backing.

Some mosaic tiles are held together by a paper facing. The tiles are fixed in the usual way, then the facing paper is peeled off once the adhesive has set. Soak a sponge with warm water and wet the tiles. Ease off the paper, starting from a corner. Finally, grout the tiles.

FITTING MOSAIC TILES

1 If the sheet of mosaic tiles has a net backing, apply adhesive directly to the wall.

2 Bed the sheets in by tapping with a mallet on a piece of wood covered with carpet.

3 Finally, grout the tiles. Wipe off the excess and leave to dry completely.

TILING CORNERS AND RECESSES

Although some tiling jobs are relatively simple, if using only whole tiles to create a splashback, for example, many are more challenging. If tiling more than one wall or a wall with a door or window, you need to know how to fit tiles around corners and awkward angles. Dealing with these situations requires more thought and planning to ensure a professional result.

INTERNAL CORNERS

At internal corners, the edges of the tiles of one wall should be allowed to overlap those of the other wall, producing a neat grouted joint. Normally, the tiles will be arranged symmetrically on each wall, almost certainly leading to cut tiles at the corner. If, however, complete tiles fit into the corner on one wall, make these overlap the cut tiles on the other wall, as this will produce a neater join. On a narrow return wall in an alcove or recess, it may be better to use whole tiles along the external corner and place narrow cut tiles at the internal corner, where they will be less noticeable.

EXTERNAL CORNERS

Special care should be taken when tiling around external corners, as any mistakes will be immediately apparent. A neat solution is to insert a strip of edge trim down the

FINISHING AN INTERNAL CORNER

1 On internal corners, place the smallest cut tiles in position first, furthest back as shown. Butter the back of the slightly larger tile.

2 Place the tile into position. Apply pressure and remove excess adhesive with a damp cloth or sponge.

corner. Fix the trim with adhesive first, then tile up to it on both walls. Take care when setting out the battens (furring strips) on each wall that they are aligned perfectly so that the rows of tiles will be even. You could also finish off an external corner with purpose-made border tiles or a wooden moulding with a painted finish.

FITTING AN EXTERNAL CORNER

1 Fix the single-edge (or double-edge) corner trim in place first.

2 Choose a colour to match your tiles, then line up the two lines of tiles.

ABOVE To finish external corners neatly, use tiles with rounded glazed edges.

Window areas

There are likely to be lots of awkward gaps to fill around a window, especially one set in a reveal. The secret of success is to follow a logical order of work and break the job down into manageable sections. Carry out a dry run to ensure that the arrangement of the tiles will be aesthetically pleasing.

Tile up to the window reveal first, taking care when you are cutting tiles so that they fit neatly. For L-shaped formations, mark in the outline with a chinagraph (wax) pencil and cut out the waste with a tile saw from the outside edge working to the centre.

Score the upright section and discard the waste. Work on the sill portion of the reveal next, leaving the sides and top until last.

For the neatest finish, position tiles with rounded or glazed edges to the front, or fit edge trim around the reveal, and fit cut tiles against the window frame. Take particular care to align tiles within the reveal with those on the main wall.

Tile the sides of the window reveal next, followed by the top section. To tile the top of the reveal, you will first need to construct a temporary wooden support to hold the tiles in place while the adhesive dries.

To make a feature of the window area you could create a frame-effect with attractive border tiles. This effect can be extended around the room at sill level to form a striking dado (chair) rail. Embossed tiles can look particularly effective when used in this way.

As ceramic border tiles can be quite expensive, aim to choose a design that will stand the test of time. Alternatively, experiment with mosaic tiles to create faux dado and picture rails for a smaller outlay.

Tiling around a window

1 Mark the outline and cut from the outside edge to the centre.

2 Tile the window sill portion next. Position the cut portions of half tiles nearest the wall.

3 Ensure all tiles align within the recess with those on the main expanse of the wall.

4 All the grout lines should match up exactly on a finished window recess.

ABOVE Find the mid-point between two windows and let your first tile line up with this.

FIXING ACCESSORIES AND GROUTING

The luxury of having a soap dish or toothbrush holder just where you want it can far outweigh the inconvenience of having to drill holes in a ceramic tile to install it. However, special tiles with pre-fixed accessories are a boon for beginners. Grouting is less daunting for the novice tiler, but it should be approached with the same thoroughness as all the preceding stages.

DRILLING HOLES

Drilling into tiles can be daunting for beginners, and while it is not particularly difficult, it is best avoided if there is an alternative. If a lot of time and effort has been spent creating a flawless tiled surface, it can be demoralizing to deal with a cracked tile or a hole that is too large as a result of a drifting drill bit. However, if there is no other option, following the technique described here will make the process a lot less painful.

It is also possible to buy accessory tiles that match the colour and dimensions of some ranges of tiles. These have bathroom fittings already in place, such as tooth mug brackets, toothbrush holders, soap dishes and toilet-roll holders.

FIXING AN ACCESSORY TILE

Leave a tile out of the appropriate row and clean any traces of adhesive.

After 24 hours, apply fresh adhesive to the back of the accessory tile and place it in the gap. Use masking tape to hold the tile in place until the adhesive is dry.

DRILLING INTO TILES

If you have to drill your own fixing holes, you can buy a special tile bit that will cut through the glaze with ease. Alternatively, a masonry bit can be used, although it is wise to break through the glaze first by tapping lightly with the point of a masonry nail. A little planning will also make the job go smoothly.

Drilling will create a lot of dust, which can discolour adjacent grout. To minimize the problem, have a helper hold the nozzle of a vacuum cleaner near the hole as you drill.

Decide exactly where you want your accessory to be and mark the spot clearly with a chinagraph pencil. Place a piece of masking tape

MAKING HOLES

1 Masking tape will stop the drill bit from slipping on the surface of the tile.

2 There are proprietary fittings that prevent drill slippage and keep the hole square.

3 Push a rawl plug into the wall beyond the back of the tile to prevent any splitting.

over the area to be drilled to stop the drill bit from slipping on the shiny surface. Mark the position of the hole clearly on the tape. Line up the bit carefully and drill through the tile and into the wall. You can now buy a fitting which will help you to drill accurately. To use it, take the sticky-back plastic off the fitting, position it where you want to drill,

ighten the ccessory, as

e gaps rout. Leave a

suitable interval for the tile adhesive to dry, typically 24 hours, before applying the grout. It can be purchased in powder form for mixing with water, or ready-mixed. Remember to use a waterproof grout in a kitchen and bathroom.

Apply the grout with a squeegee or damp sponge, working it well into the tile joints. Cover an area of about 1sq m (11sq ft) with each application of grout.

Do not allow the grout to dry on the surface of the tiles, as it will be difficult to remove. Wipe off excess as you work with a damp cloth. If you prefer a concave finish to the grout, run a piece of dowel or a

ABOVE You can now buy specially made tools for tidying sealant. Use a sealant specially formulated for the job.

proprietary grout shaper gently along each joint. Allow the grout to dry, then wipe over the tiles with a damp sponge. Finally, polish with a cloth for a gleaming finish.

1 Use a squeegee or sponge to work the grout well into the tile joints.

2 While the grout is moist, wipe excess off the face of the tiles with a damp sponge or cloth.

GROUT WHITENERS

If grouting becomes discoloured, whitening products are available that are simply painted on to create sparkling new grout lines. Clean the area well and allow to dry before applying the new finish. Coloured grout can look very dramatic, especially between white tiles. However, some types are not suitable for use over waterproof grout. Always check the manufacturer's instructions.

3 Press a piece of dowelling gently into each grout line to give a neat finish.

4 Finish the job by applying sealant to the gap between the tiles and basin or bath.

ABOVE For a good finish, use a special grout shaper to joint the tiles.

INDEX

PICTURE CREDITS

The publisher would like to thank the following for permission to reproduce their images in this book: Axminster Power Tool Centre: 11bc; 12tc. DIY Photo Library: 45bl. Simon Gilham: 42bl. HSS Tool Hire: 12c; 13t, c, r; 43br. Thompson's (Ronseal): 45br.